"Evelyn Forget and Ha̶̶̶̶̶̶̶̶̶̶̶̶̶̶̶̶̶̶̶̶̶̶̶̶̶̶ and compassionate case for basic income as a necessary element of a fair society with opportunity for all. They address head-on the oft-heard criticism that basic income recipients cannot be trusted to spend unconditional dollars wisely. On the contrary, basic income in combination with other social supports is a ticket to escape debilitating life situations that befall some persons, whether that be incarceration, addiction, dependency on foster care, disability, violent surroundings or precarious work. They present convincing evidence that an unconditional basic income will be used productively to invest in the betterment of recipients and their dependents, and therefore to the benefit of society. The narrative draws on first-hand accounts of those with lived experience of being trapped in poverty and is utterly persuasive."

—Robin Boadway, Professor of Economics Emeritus, Queen's University

"Evelyn Forget and Hannah Owczar have written a page-turner with a simple but critical message. Society today is experiencing a trust divide, with half the population setting rules they mistrust the other half to follow. The result is a social support system designed to control rather than help those in need. Fuelled by powerful testimonies from individuals experiencing the complex web of social policies first-hand, *Radical Trust* gives the reader deep insight in how a system rooted in distrust constantly fails the very people it is meant to help. Forget and Owczar offer an attractive solution: how about giving each individual a basic income and simply trusting them to use it to better their own lives as they—not we—see fit?"

—Jurgen De Wispelaere, PhD., Assistant Professor, Stockholm School of Economics in Riga

"This book is a must read for all those who wish to be informed about how a basic income would contribute to a more just and equitable society. If a basic income were implemented, it would not be a panacea, but it would improve the lives of many marginalized and struggling Canadians considerably. Forget and Owczar illustrate this with empathy and humility, providing detailed analyses of the challenges faced and the (inadequate) services and supports currently available to those who are aging out of foster care, leaving prison, homeless, struggling with addictions, living with a disability, or precariously employed."

—Elizabeth (Mandy) Kay-Raining Bird,
PhD & Chair, Basic Income Nova Scotia

"Radical Trust is essential reading for anyone in Canada with hopes for a more just and equitable society. In offering basic income as one potential solution to poverty and income insecurity, Evelyn Forget and Hannah Owczar compellingly ask readers a simple question: what would happen if we trusted people to make decisions about their own lives?

Through a seamless narrative weaving together personal accounts with existing research, Forget and Owczar shed light on how a basic income guarantee could change so many peoples' lives for the better - especially those furthest on the margins. From those struggling with substance use disorder to formerly-incarcerated individuals to youth aging out of care, the authors expertly and compassionately build the case for a country where no one is left behind. Radical Trust is a must-read for those curious about the potential effects of a basic income, including for children and youth. Policymakers, researchers, and advocates will be better for reading it."

—Chloe Halpenny and Kendal David, co-founders and co-chairs,
Basic Income Canada Youth Network

"This book paints a disturbing, intimate human portrait of trust that is radically absent in policies that should help people but don't, where rights and diversity are undermined by paternalism and privilege. A basic income can change that, quickly."
—Sheila Regehr, Chair, Basic Income Canada Network and former federal public servant and Executive Director of the National Council of Welfare

"Every candidate and voter should read Radical Trust: Basic Income for Complicated Lives and every legislator and policymaker should be guided by it. With every page, Evelyn Forget and Hannah Owczar lay out the stark and disturbing realities of the increasing economic, racial, health and social inequalities experienced by the least privileged in our country. They also clearly and concisely point the way forward out of the economic, social and health crises and massive systemic inequality laid bare by COVID-19 and the patchwork of federal, provincial and municipal responses. Radical Trust urges Canadians to embrace values of generosity, kindness and willingness to assist more than just the people who are currently judged as deserving of support. They reveal how everyone will benefit from basic income initiatives in no small part because of the ways they leave nobody behind, provide a concrete step toward reconciliation with Indigenous Peoples and insure against current and future unpredictable life events."

We owe the authors a huge debt of gratitude for this invaluable, insightful, disturbing yet hopeful and inspirational book."
—The Honourable Kim Pate, C.M., Senator

Copyright © 2021 Evelyn L. Forget & Hannah Owczar

ARP Books (Arbeiter Ring Publishing)
205-70 Arthur Street
Winnipeg, Manitoba
Treaty 1 Territory and Historic Métis Nation Homeland Canada R3B 1G7
arpbooks.org

Cover design by Leslie Supnet.
Interior layout by Relish New Brand Experience.
Printed and bound in Canada by Imprimerie Gauvin on certified FSC ® paper.

Copyright Notice
This book is fully protected under the copyright laws of Canada and all other countries of the Copyright Union and is subject to royalty.

ARP Books acknowledges the generous support of the Manitoba Arts Council and the Canada Council for the Arts for our publishing program. We acknowledge the financial support of the Government of Canada and the Province of Manitoba through the Book Publishing Tax Credit and the Book Publisher Marketing Assistance Program of Manitoba Culture, Heritage, and Tourism.

Library and Archives Canada Cataloguing in Publication

Title: Radical trust : basic income for complicated lives / Evelyn L. Forget & Hannah Owczar.
Names: Forget, Evelyn L., 1956- author. | Owczar, Hannah, author.
Description: Includes index.
Identifiers: Canadiana (print) 20210276355 | Canadiana (ebook) 20210277742 | ISBN 9781927886472 (softcover) | ISBN 9781927886489 (ebook)
Subjects: LCSH: Basic income—Canada. | LCSH: Income maintenance programs—Canada. | LCSH: Social security—Canada. | LCSH: Economic security—Canada. | LCSH: Income distribution—Canada. | LCSH: Poverty—Canada.
Classification: LCC HC120.I5 F69 2021 | DDC 362.5/820971—dc23

Radical Trust
Basic Income for Complicated Lives

Evelyn L. Forget & Hannah Owczar
ARP Books | Winnipeg MB

This book is dedicated to everyone who shared their stories with us, who pointed out our mistakes and blind spots with far more patience than we deserved, and who really tried to help us shift our focus and see the world from different perspectives. We hope you aren't disappointed.

And,

To RAL, for everything, from Evelyn

To Mom, Dad, and Adam, for making this world a better place, from Hannah

Contents

Introduction 9

1 Playing by the Rules 16
2 Leaving Foster Care for Life as an Adult 36
3 Walking with Bear Clan Patrol: Substance Use and Basic Income 48
4 Life After Prison 60
5 Trapped in the Precariat 72
6 Living with Disabilities 88
7 Violence Against Women and Gender-Diverse People 103
8 Basic Income, Reconciliation, and the Way Forward 119

A Reader's Guide 138

Additional Resources 149

Interviewees 151

Index 155

Introduction

When COVID-19 swept across the world in the early weeks of 2020, few of us could imagine how dramatically all our lives would change. Face masks and social distancing soon became routine, but there were indications of more profound adjustments on the horizon. Children staying at home because schools and daycares closed and people dying in nursing homes forced us to recognize how much our pre-pandemic lives depended on someone providing care work that was too often taken for granted. The invisible and unpaid work of family members expanded, and people living in nursing homes suffered the consequences of an entire sector built on underpaid support workers with little job security and no guaranteed sick leave, travelling by public transportation from one hot spot to another.

In Canada and elsewhere, workplaces and businesses closed in response to the declaration on March 11, 2020, by the World Health Organization that this novel coronavirus constituted a global pandemic. Some people were able to work from home with the assistance of technology, but many lost their jobs and recognized for the first time how precarious their own economic security was and how precarious the lives of their neighbours and family members were. People who never expected to be without work and in need of government support found they were unable to pay their rents and mortgages and worried about how they would be able to buy groceries.

The social safety net that we thought would protect us had gaping holes. Many people who lost their jobs found that they did not qualify for support from Employment Insurance or would receive too little to meet their most basic needs. They tasted just a little of the economic insecurity that characterizes the lives of people who are often invisible in our society: those without stable housing, those who live with substance use or disabilities, those who are criminalized, and those whose forms of labour are not acknowledged as work, or whose rights as labourers are routinely ignored. But the government was unwilling to allow armies of middle-class workers to suffer and, in a matter of weeks, introduced the Canadian Emergency Response Benefit (CERB), which promised to pay those who lost work during the pandemic $2,000 a month—more than twice the amount an individual could expect from provincial income assistance. The CERB was carefully designed to exclude the most vulnerable people in our society; support was conditional on $5,000 of earned income in the previous twelve months, which disqualified most people who relied on provincial income assistance or disability support.

At the same time, the armies of low-paid workers who keep our economies running continued to work, often at significant health risk. While health-care workers gained a lot of attention for their important roles on the front lines of the pandemic, there were many others, including food production workers, supermarket cashiers, and cleaners, who continued to provide essential services. Even during pre-COVID times, many people earned too little to be able to raise themselves out of poverty. For a brief time during early COVID days, they were called "heroes" by the media and governments, and some received temporary bonuses, but there was no permanent improvement to the terms and conditions under which they worked.

All of this reanimated the conversation in Canada about a guaranteed basic income. Over the following months, the Senate

Finance Committee, the Steelworkers Union, 4,000 organizations and individuals representing women, organizations representing 75,000 artists, the Canadian Chamber of Commerce, groups of academics, health-care providers, several faith groups, and many more indicated their support for basic income, and wrote policy briefs and letters to the prime minister asking that a permanent basic income be part of the pandemic recovery.

Before the 2020 pandemic, most middle-class Canadians could ignore the pockets of persistent poverty in our midst and the growing economic insecurity associated with precarious labour. They could pretend that our social safety net was adequate and that everyone had the same opportunity to live with dignity. If someone struggled financially, it was easy for most Canadians to assume that they must, somehow, be responsible for their own situation. This assumption generated social programs like provincial income assistance, which is a program of last resort that provides levels of support well below the poverty line, and imposes onerous conditions and constraints on recipients that are intended to force them to find a job or someone else to support them. Income support programs in Canada were designed with the explicit purpose of "creating incentives" to encourage those who rely on these programs to behave in ways consistent with the dominant culture—for their own good, of course.

The pandemic offered an opportunity to view economic insecurity from a different perspective. Basic income treats people as adults and trusts them to make their own decisions about how to live their lives. This simple change alters everything. Basic income is not a radical proposition; its benefits have been demonstrated time and again, and studies have shown that Canada has the financial and technical capacity to offer a guaranteed income to everyone. However, trusting one another is radical.

Basic income rests on the concept of *radical trust*—trust in our neighbours, friends, and relatives, even when they make decisions different from the ones we might prefer. A basic income would be available to everyone whose income is below the poverty line, without condition. Advice on budgeting, job training, or parenting might be provided for people who want it, but their basic income would not depend on participating in programs or complying with the advice that is offered.

The purpose of this book was, originally, to amplify the voices of some of the people who are not well served by the income support programs that have been cobbled together over the years. We imagined a chapter on formerly incarcerated people, expecting them to talk about the difficulties they faced as they tried to rebuild their lives and their families. We imagined another on young people aging out of foster care, expecting them to list the many ways they struggled to find the resources they need to live. Perhaps we'd have another chapter on people who use alcohol or drugs, focusing on the absence of safe consumption sites and their experiences with criminalization. Our goal was to borrow stories from people willing to share them—stories that would illustrate the complex lives of people who were struggling—and to show how a basic income would better serve their needs.

As we started to collect these stories, though, we found an astonishingly generous community of people who were willing to help us learn—really learn. And we did learn so much more than we expected, but we also began to recognize how ignorant we still are. Many of the stories in these pages are about people who could fit into any one of our chapters. People who live on the streets very often have done so from a very young age, when they left difficult situations in foster care or in their families. Substance use is the way that many are first criminalized. Some people had their first experience of incarceration while they were in foster care, and many women were first trafficked as children. So many experienced such profound and continuous violence, both psychological and physical, that it became normalized; they couldn't tell us about the "first time" they were victimized because they couldn't remember a time when they hadn't been. Many of the people who shared their stories are people of colour, Indigenous people, and queer people—people who don't identify with the dominant culture. They told us how public services and supports are experienced as systems of coercion that fail to address their unique needs. All are, or have been, people who did not have enough money to meet their basic needs.

During COVID-19, it became a cliché for governments to tell us that "we are all in this together." Yet it was obvious from the outset that the effects of the pandemic were not the same for everyone. Some people "self-isolated" in 2,500-square-foot homes packed with every entertainment device anyone could want. When schools reopened, some had to think hard about whether they would participate in a "learning pod" by hiring a teacher with friends and neighbours in their "bubble" or step out of the workforce to care for young children until the pandemic passed, or to take a chance on the schools. Others had dramatically different experiences, working in meat-packing plants that could not guarantee their safety but threatened their eligibility for the CERB if they refused to work. Many people searched desperately for adequate child care when schools and daycares closed, but their jobs required them to continue working.

People who had already been struggling faced even greater hardship. When food banks couldn't meet their needs, some wondered how they would continue to survive on provincial disability support that paid less than half the rate that displaced workers received. Those who used drugs could not access the safe consumption sites they depended upon, and interruptions to the supply chain made their usual sources even more hazardous. Some had mental health issues that were exacerbated by isolation, while others wondered how they could maintain safe distances in shelters or spent more nights outside on the streets as these same shelters limited the spaces available. Those with children but without the resources to pay for reliable Internet wondered how online education could work.

The stories people shared with us are important and we are grateful for the generosity of our witnesses. The authors of this book struggled with the content of some of these stories as we tried to understand a little better how we fit into the narrative. We write from a place of privilege that isn't always comfortable to acknowledge. Neither of us has ever experienced, or even witnessed, some of the experiences people told us about. It would be easy for us to portray ourselves as neutral observers, claiming to "give a platform" to the voices of other people even as we used their stories to make a case for our own policy goals. That struggle is part of a larger injustice: we have benefited all our lives and in many ways from the systems that oppress other people—the people who shared their stories in this book.

Our purpose in writing this book is to help other people like us, who occupy positions of privilege and sometimes have the ear of policy-makers, to understand why a basic income is a necessary feature of a just society. We are most emphatically not speaking for the people in this book; some of them support the idea of a basic income, others do not, and many had never thought about the question. We are not giving people a voice; they have their own voices. We are writing from our perspective. We've tried to pass along the stories our witnesses shared with us honestly, but perspective matters. We do not claim that our perspective has not influenced the way we present the content of these chapters. Many of our witnesses are Indigenous; we talk about reconciliation in the final chapter, but we talk about it from our own perspective as members of settler families with all the limitations that identity necessarily entails. We were given permission to share the personal stories of witnesses in this book, and we gave each participant the opportunity to review and approve their direct quotes. Most interviews were done in person over the course of the past two years, starting in 2019. Many of the people we interviewed are from Manitoba, but their stories have national implications. We tried to use the language our witnesses used when we told their stories. We are still learning.

We hope this book is useful to the many Canadians who worry about the growing disparities in our communities and want to understand better the lives of some of our friends, neighbours, and relatives who survive without the resources they need to live with dignity. Learning, when it is honest and deep, is both transformative and deeply uncomfortable. We hope some of these stories make readers uncomfortable—uncomfortable enough to pay attention to policy debates, to challenge acquaintances who offer easy opinions about the lives of people they don't understand and facile solutions to complex problems. We try to deepen that discomfort by posing a series of questions for reflection and discussion in reading groups or seminar rooms. We hope these questions challenge us to examine the way we understand the communities in which we live. We hope they also ask us to be honest about how willing we are to share with one another. We've included some resources for further learning and opportunities for engagement.

The people who have generously shared their stories with us know what it means to live complicated lives. When your life is complicated, there are no simple fixes that will solve all your problems. That includes basic income. Basic income is not a silver bullet; it is a human right. As you read these stories, read with one question in mind: Would this person's life be better or worse if they had predictable access to a guaranteed income sufficient to meet their daily needs?

Canada has the resources and technical capacity to offer a basic income; we believe that justice requires no less than an honest attempt to ensure that all of us have what we need to live modest lives with dignity.

1
Playing by the Rules

> "Remember the Golden Rule! Whoever who has the gold, makes the rules!"—The Wizard of ID

The French philosopher Jean-Jacques Rousseau said the same thing, more or less, 250 years ago.[1] People who rise to positions of authority in any society are usually people who share the dominant values of that society. They are people who design curricula for the schools, sentence people in courtrooms, put on police uniforms, create non-governmental organizations, run clinics, write newspaper editorials, organize food banks, run for office, and decide who to hire or fire. At every stage in their lives, they interact with institutions and authorities that share and reaffirm their values, and so they can live their lives without constantly reflecting on the rules of the game.

By contrast, people who do not share these values bump up against all these invisible rules all the time. They might be Indigenous people with different world views, newcomers to Canada, racialized people, those who do not conform to traditional gender roles, or people with low incomes in a society that values financial success. Throughout their lives, they interact with people and institutions that seem to expect something from them, but the expectations are never quite clear because the rules of the game are all implicit.

These two groups of people regularly come into contact with one another in the context of the many different government programs that offer financial support or other services to people who live in Canada. The policy-makers, caseworkers who design, implement, and evaluate these programs are ... of the dominant culture who collectively control the resources that will be made available. The people who rely on such services represent a much broader range of people with a much broader range of perspectives on the way the world works. As a consequence, many of these programs attempt to "educate," "incentivize," and, when these fail, coerce recipients into changing their behaviour.

The Existing Social Safety Net

There are hundreds of different support programs in Canada, offered by federal, provincial, municipal, and Indigenous governments. These programs are uncoordinated, with different application processes, regulations, and eligibility requirements. Some offer cash, either as direct payments or as income tax refunds, while others offer services such as extended health care or job training. Some require recipients to have paid into the system, such as through Employment Insurance and the Canada Pension Plan, while others are based on different assessments of need. The very complexity of the system ensures that many people do not receive the benefits to which they are entitled. Some fall into the gaps between programs, while others are held in limbo as different levels of government argue with one another about who has responsibility for an applicant.

Each particular program is designed to encourage those who can work for pay to do so as quickly as possible. Programs designed for those who cannot work are encumbered with regulations designed to ensure that no one who could work "takes advantage." The result is a complex bureaucratic system burdened with paperwork and run by a system of caseworkers whose primary task is to ensure that clients follow the vast array of regulations governing each program. Payouts are miserly to ensure that everyone has a strong incentive to get a job as quickly as possible.

I: Incomes for the Old and the Young

Neither children nor people over 65 are expected to work for pay in Canada, so these groups of people are entitled to receive unconditional support: the parents of children under 18 receive the Canada Child Benefit (CCB), which is based on the age of the child and the income of the family, and people over 65 receive Old Age Security (OAS) and, if their income is low enough, the Guaranteed Income Supplement (GIS). The GIS and CCB are different from other forms of income support because the benefit is guaranteed and unconditional, as long as an applicant meets the age and income requirements. Recipients don't have to meet any additional requirements, such as demonstrating that they are actively seeking employment. They don't have to sell all their assets and apply early for any pensions they might one day be entitled to receive, and they don't have to demonstrate that there is no one else who can provide the income support they need. Their income, in that sense, is guaranteed.

II: Income Replacement for People with Disabilities

Working-age people with disabilities might not be expected to work, but in order to receive provincial disability support, they must demonstrate to the satisfaction of the authorities that they have a "genuine" disability that interferes with their ability to work. This entails a report from a health-care practitioner that offers a diagnosis and prognosis for the condition, and a second report on how the condition interferes with the activities of daily living. Eligibility rules are so bureaucratic and difficult to interpret that a number of non-profit agencies have emerged to advise applicants about how best to apply and to advise medical practitioners about how to complete the forms to maximize the probability of success. Qualification is not automatic, and two people with similar conditions may find themselves treated differently, depending on the discretion of authorities and the skill of the practitioner who completed the forms. Recipients may have to requalify on a regular basis to demonstrate that their condition has not abated. People with disabilities might also qualify for federal disability support through the Canada Pension Plan, if they have worked in the past, and many will have access to an array of income tax credits and deductions

Additional supports such as extended health care are often tied to provincial disability support. This can act as a barrier for people whose condition varies over time. If they work when they are able, they might lose supports that later become necessary if their condition worsens.

III: Income Replacement for Working-Age People

Working-age people without disabilities are subject to income-support programs designed to distinguish between those who want to work and those who do not want to work. The programs are intended to "incentivize" working in the paid labour market and "disincentivize" not working for a wage. The least punitive form of income support for working-age people is Employment Insurance (EI), which is a national program and entirely financed by contributions from workers and employers. An applicant is eligible for EI only if they have worked a specified number of qualifying hours in the previous twelve months or since the last time they received EI payments. Before the COVID-19 pandemic, the number of qualifying hours depended on the strength of the labour market in the region of the country in which an applicant lived, so that in high-employment areas they must have worked more hours than in low-employment areas. The amount an applicant would receive was set at 55 per cent of insurable earnings, to a maximum of $573 a week, but low-income workers would receive much less. There was no minimum. Support under EI was temporary: the maximum period of support varied depending on time worked and the strength of the labour market in the region, with applicants in high-employment areas of the country receiving support for a maximum of fourteen weeks.

In order to receive support, applicants were required to be available for work, demonstrate that they had actively sought work, and be willing to accept any reasonable job offer. These requirements exclude people who are at home caring for family members with disabilities or young children and those who are engaged in education without explicit permission. All of this is designed to ensure that people who can work find jobs as quickly as possible.

When COVID-19 entered the picture, it was immediately apparent that EI could not meet the needs of millions of Canadians displaced by the pandemic. Children at home after elementary schools and daycares were shut down by public health authorities needed care, but EI required parents to be available for work. People were displaced from their jobs when businesses closed, but if they turned to EI, some found that they had amassed too few insurable hours to qualify or, if they did qualify, they received far too little support to meet their basic needs. Some were self-employed and not covered by EI, and still others worked non-standard contracts in the gig economy, which didn't allow them to qualify. Displaced workers would have recognized just how broken our social safety net had become if the government had not developed a set of emergency benefits, such as the Canada Emergency Response Benefit (CERB), which temporarily plugged the gaps in EI. The CERB effectively allowed displaced workers to continue to ignore the plight of those who receive far lower levels of support and far higher levels of scrutiny on provincial income assistance.

Working-age adults who don't qualify for EI can turn to provincial income assistance, which is, like disability support, a program of last resort. Depending on the province, this might be called "welfare," "employment and income assistance," or "social assistance." Program details vary by province, but in every case, recipients are eligible for levels of support far below the poverty line. Applying for the program requires individuals to meet with a caseworker, bringing with them evidence of their earnings and expenses, including rent receipts. The amount of property a recipient can own is strictly limited, and applicants are required to sell anything over the specified amount—including things like snowmobiles or boats or cars worth more than a specific amount—to support themselves before provincial income assistance can be offered. They are required to apply for any other programs for which they might qualify, such as the Canada Pension Plan, because provincial income assistance is a program of last resort. Similarly, applicants are required to pursue any child support they may be owed, whether they want contact with former partners or not. Caseworkers can check with banks and landlords to verify the information provided and, during the application process, a caseworker can arrive at an applicant's home at any time, without notice, to inspect the premises.

The amount of support received is based on family size, but it is not formulaic. There are many special allowances and restrictions that can come into play at any time. Even a gift of groceries from a family member will be counted as income and the benefit may be reduced. Every month, there is paperwork to be completed and, if it is late, a payment may be delayed or denied. Applicants are required to provide any information requested at any time, including birth certificates already on file, details of custody arrangements, changes of address, and any changes in the people living in the apartment. Failure to report can result in denial of benefits or fraud charges. The caseworker is given the primary task of policing clients to protect taxpayers from fraud.

The result is that a recipient sometimes doesn't know how much money they will receive in any month. Even if the benefit is paid in full and on time, it is insufficient to pay even modest rents or living expenses, forcing recipients into precarious housing. As in the case of disability support, there are additional benefits tied to income support, including Pharmacare in some provinces. Even though the entire system is designed to ensure that support is offered only to applicants who are willing to work, these tied benefits make it difficult for recipients to take a job because they lose all these additional benefits when they no longer qualify for income support.

The entire process is one of distrust and intrusion. Provincial income assistance condemns recipients to a life of social scrutiny, food banks, shelters, and charities. This is quite different from the experience of CERB applicants, who were offered a simplified online application portal (with telephone access to administrators for those without Internet access) and were required merely to state their earnings each month, with the promise that overpayments would be rectified when they filed their income tax. Workers displaced by COVID-19 were offered dignity and trust.

The Basic Income Alternative

Basic income is not just another income assistance program; it is designed to allow individuals to make their own decisions about their own lives, unlike provincial income assistance, which is freighted with bureaucratic oversight. Basic income is a guarantee that everyone will have enough money to live a modest life with dignity. No one will be forced to survive on an income far below the poverty line, as is currently the case for all recipients of provincial income assistance and disability support.

When people talk about basic income, they sometimes mean different things. A Universal Basic Income (UBI) gives everyone, rich or poor, the same amount of money each month, and the government relies on a progressive tax system to recover some of the money paid to those with high incomes. A UBI has never found much traction in Canada, largely because of the cost associated with sending money to high-income people who don't need it. Nevertheless, people sometimes use the term "UBI" loosely, as a way of referring in need of support. That idea, however, is deeply rooted in North American society among people of different ideological backgrounds. For example, the Brookings Institution is an American organization that conducts research in the areas of economics, governance, and foreign policy. It has a strong reputation for unbiased research, with a slight tendency to favour left or liberal public policy. In 2013, Ron Haskins, one of its Senior Fellows, penned an article entitled "Three Simple Rules Poor Teens Should Follow to Join the Middle Class."[4] He claimed that many poor children come from families that don't offer them the support that middle-class children receive, and, therefore, they begin kindergarten well behind their peers. Many fall further behind as they get older, and most never catch up. He noted that poor children are more likely to make decisions that are associated with poverty as adults: to drop out of school, become teen parents, join gangs, and break the law. The solution to poverty, he argued, is quite simple: "politicians, schoolteachers and administrators, community leaders, ministers and parents [must] drill into children the message that in a free society, they enter adulthood with three major responsibilities: at least finish high school, get a full-time job and wait until age 21 to get married and have children."

The research is valid only as far as it goes: among adults who have graduated from high school, work full time, and wait until they are in committed relationships to have children, only 2 per cent live in poverty. However, it misses the most important points: the outcomes of one generation determine the opportunities of the next; and, joining the middle class, however one might choose to define that, is not a universal aspiration.

Children born into the middle class often make the same kinds of decisions that children born into financially vulnerable families make, but they face dramatically different consequences. A child who struggles in the early years of elementary school will fall further and further behind unless they get additional support. Help is available within the school system, but a persistent parent with the confidence that comes with education and money can help ensure their child receives whatever support is available. A child born into a financially stable family may also have access to tutors and psychological testing outside the school system. By contrast, a child born into a family working hard just to make ends meet may change schools several times because of housing instability, losing the opportunity to form strong attachments with teachers and to develop a consistent approach to addressing learning deficits.

Financially vulnerable families are also more prone to come in contact with Child and Family Services agencies (CFS) than middle-class families. Abuse and neglect occur at all income levels, but poor parents (and especially poor mothers) are more likely to find themselves in situations that attract the attention of authorities. Good-quality child care is expensive and not always accessible to parents who work at jobs with irregular hours. Parents who have jobs that require them to be available on short notice or to take varying shifts may instead rely on friends or family to provide care. Sometimes this is a wonderful solution for a family, while at other times it is a matter of necessity and not a choice that would be made if alternatives were available.

Children from all backgrounds who miss school or have behaviour issues will often attract the attention of well-meaning teachers and administrators who are required to call CFS if they fear a child is being mistreated. The consequences, however, differ for low-income families from those for families with more adequate income. Having come to the attention of CFS, a parent without reliable transportation, stable housing, or a livable income will have a much harder time demonstrating to a middle-class caseworker that they are capable of caring adequately for their child. A caseworker who finds no food in the house will use their judgment to determine whether the situation is one of poverty or neglect. If a child is taken into care, the results often spiral downwards. While the stated goal of CFS is family reunification, circumstances conspire against this for financially vulnerable families. W[hen no] longer living with a family, the family will lose t[he Child] Benefit and suffer a reduction of provincial income assistance. This makes it harder for the family to afford the rent on a safe apartment with space for a child, or to demonstrate the capacity to provide adequate care if the child were to come home. Precarious housing and unpredictable work schedules make it challenging to reunite the family.

The relationships among CFS, educational outcomes, and poverty are complex. Children who come into contact with CFS are more likely to have been born too soon and too small, which is sometimes associated with persistent health and learning issues, and often the result of maternal poverty that makes access to regular prenatal care and a nourishing diet during pregnancy challenging. A study by Manitoba Centre for Health Policy found that children born into families that struggle financially are much more likely to be taken into the care of CFS. Sixty-nine per cent of children taken into care come from families receiving provincial income assistance, compared with 12 per cent of children who never had CFS contact. More than 40 per cent of children taken into care were born to mothers who were less than 18 years old when their first child was born, compared with 6.8 per cent of children with no CFS contact. Over 13 per cent of children taken into care had mothers who reported substance use during pregnancy, compared with 1.6 per cent of children with no CFS contact.[5]

Having come into contact with CFS, a child is less likely to do well on standardized tests throughout their time in school, and less likely to graduate from high school. At the age of 5, 47 per cent of children in care are judged school-ready, compared with 76 per cent of other children. By grade three, 49 per cent of children in care are competent in math, compared with 80 per cent of other children. By grade eight, 49 per cent of children in care are competent in reading and writing, compared with 85 per cent of other children. Children receiving care from CFS fall further and further behind. Only 33 per cent of children in care graduate from high school, compared with 89 per cent of other children.[6]

There is also a relationship among poverty, CFS, and the youth justice system. Canada has a very high rate of children in the care of CFS, children in custody, and children involved in both systems. Among Canadian provinces, Manitoba has the highest rates of child apprehension by both systems. Another study by the Manitoba Centre for Health Policy examined the characteristics of children involved in the youth justice system and discovered that the strongest predictor of being charged with a crime was being in the care of CFS. The type of placement also mattered; children in group homes were more likely to be taken into custody than those in foster homes.[7] More than a third of the children who had been in the care of CFS were accused of a crime, and almost two-thirds didn't graduate from high school.

None of the statistics that describe the lives of vulnerable children tell us what the ultimate cause of their difficulties might be. Few of these children face only a single challenge. Some face lives with physical and mental challenges from the time of their births. Others are born healthy, but changes in custody arrangements and stints in CFS care disrupt healthy preschool development. Some are neglected or abused. Still others do well as young children but drift into trouble as they get older. In many cases, poverty is a fellow traveller. Poverty constrains the decisions that parents can make, even before a child is born, and the opportunities they can offer their children; a parent's own childhood poverty influences their decisions and the behaviours they can model for a child.

People of all backgrounds and at all income levels sometimes make risky decisions. The consequences, however, are so much worse for those who begin life in difficult circumstances than for those born into more fortunate lives. Being Indigenous in a society that devalues Indigenous people or being born to a young mother or into a poor family doesn't cause anyone to commit a crime, join a gang, or drop out of school. Some people who began life in challenging circumstances go on to make astounding achievements in many fields. Starting life in difficult circumstances does, however, take away opportunities to recover. The authorities with whom young people come into contact will make judgments about their character based on their own experiences and biases. Someone who is imagined to come from a "good" home or a "good" family might be treated less harshly than someone from an "unstable" family, living in "precarious circumstances," or who associates with "a bad crowd."

The overrepresentation of Indigenous children in care, in poverty, and in the youth justice system is part of an undeniable legacy of colonialism in Canada. CFS and the youth justice system continue the tradition established by the residential school system and the Sixties Scoop, in which children were taken from their families and adopted out to be raised among strangers far from their home, language, and culture.[8] Today, there are more children in Canada's child-welfare systems than there were at the height of residential schools.[9] The funding received by Indigenous communities and organizations to provide services lags well behind that received by other residents of Canada,[10] and Indigenous people face racism in the context of access to public services and in society more generally.[11]

Parents make decisions that have consequences for their children, but no child chooses their parents. Even adults can make decisions only in the context of the opportunities and knowledge available to them. Their own childhood experiences, and even the experiences of their parents and grandparents and the behaviours they modelled, shape the opportunities available to adults.

Taken together, all of the various facets of deprivation make a mockery of the "three simple rules" offered by the Brookings Institution. The choices we make have some role to play in the kind of life we find ourselves living, but plain luck, good or bad, is far more significant than many of us would like to admit. So much of what happens to us is completely outside our control, especially when we are children.

Why Is It So Hard for Middle-Class People to Recognize the Structural Determinants of Poverty?

The belief that our behaviours and decisions determine what kind of lives we lead and what happens to us is pervasive, even among well-meaning people who are genuinely dedicated to improving opportunities for everyone. In Canada, most middle-class people work hard to earn the money they spend. They devote years of their lives to training for jobs, then work long hours to earn down-payments for housing and cars and to set a little aside for emergencies and for retirement. On average, according to the Organization for Economic Co-Operation and Development, Canadians work more hours each year than most western Europeans,[12] and a study from the National Bureau of Economic Research indicates that those with higher incomes tend to work more hours than those with lower incomes.[13]

Many middle-class people did not come from well-off families. Some can tell stories about parents and grandparents who arrived in Canada with few resources but a burning ambition to provide a better life for their children, and others are immigrants themselves. Some tell of the back-breaking toil their parents grew up with on prairie farms or Newfoundland fishing boats. Many work hard and celebrate hard work as the path to a better life. It is much harder to recognize that others live with different advantages and barriers.

No one is solely responsible for their successes—just as no one is solely responsible for their failures. Many well-off Canadians arrived in Canada as the children of penniless refugees after the Second World War. Others arrived from Asia with little money. Both groups brought an outsized veneration for formal education cultivated over generations. With that support behind them, their children sought out educational opportunities that some turned into professional careers. Others were born in Toronto or Montreal as the children of parents fleeing subsistence farms elsewhere in Canada, and forget that simply being born in the postwar period meant that a single adult income in a factory could provide some with a middle-class upbringing, including a house and access to all the new schools, public transportation, and public programs put in place for the children of the baby boom. That solid foundation created opportunities for long-lasting educational and professional success—for some. Still others brought their entrepreneurial vision to build businesses that prospered but forget that their success depends on the investments that society made in public education that trained their workforce, in a legal infrastructure that helped enforce their contracts, and in public services that supplemented the earnings of their employees.

Being poor is also hard work, but it's the kind of hard work that doesn't offer generous paycheques. Taking public transportation between multiple part-time, low-wage jobs requires a lot of time and effort. Coordinating quality child care that meets the needs of jobs with varying hours is not a simple task. It requires a lot of effort to take public transportation to the supermarket or to wash your clothes at a laundromat. It's hard work to find a landlord prepared to rent a decent apartment to someone who depends on provincial income assistance. When the money runs out, it's very stressful to explain to a child why they can't participate in Pizza Day at school, or why you can't provide the second pair of running shoes the school demands for gym use only. Cooking dinner takes time and money, and the less money you have, the more time it takes to find food you can afford, to create nutritious meals around food bank staples, or even to cook the dried beans, vegetables, and meat cuts you can afford.

Any one of us can fall victim to poor health, have a parent struggling with age-related issues, lose a spouse to an early and unexpected death or a marital breakdown, or, for that matter, win the lottery. Each unexpected event sets into motion a chain of events that will have lasting consequences. A fragile marriage, for example, might shatter with the stress of a child born with health problems. A parent who becomes the sole caregiver for the child might then drop out of the workforce to provide necessary care and forfeit the career they have spent years building. Housing might need to be downgraded, but living in a different neighbourhood makes accessing the informal support they had received from friends and family more difficult. Their lower income makes it harder to supplement public services, and these events follow the family for at least two generations.

By contrast, a lucky break—perhaps a friend from school who passes along information about a job opportunity that turns into a lengthy and remunerative career—can set the stage for many other "lucky breaks," such as the opportunity to pay for the coaches who can nurture your athletic daughter's dreams or the music teachers who can develop your son's talent, or the financial resources to pay for private nurses when a partner's dementia makes additional care essential.

The Policy Implications of Acknowledging Structural Forces

Every one of us lives a life that is unique. Our strengths and weaknesses, goals and fears, opportunities and constraints are different from those of everyone else, as are the accidents of fate that offer unique challenges and opportunities. However, for all of us, the reality is the same: we control some aspects of our lives and some of it is entirely out of our hands.

This reality, however, runs counter to a distinction that has dominated British and North American public policy since at least the sixteenth century—that some people deserve public support while others do not. In too many ways, it is a small step to contemporary policy debate, where "working" is still seen as the highest moral good. Those who can't work might be eligible for levels of provincial disability support that ensure they live well below the poverty line. Public policy is designed to ensure that anyone else who needs support is encouraged to work. Great amounts of energy are devoted to worrying about work disincentives that might allow someone to live without working. There is far more political support for guaranteed jobs than for guaranteed incomes, because a guaranteed job would require anyone who needs support to work hard for it, while a guaranteed income might allow someone to survive without working.

Poverty, however, is not a moral failing. No one deserves to be poor. According to the Universal Declaration of Human Rights issued by the United Nations, everyone has a fundamental right to "a standard of living adequate for the health and well-being of himself and of his family, including food, clothing, housing and medical care and necessary social services."[14] Children are entitled to "special care and assistance." The Declaration doesn't limit these rights to the middle class and people working hard to join it, or give the government the right to withhold an adequate standard of living from people who choose not to follow the three simple rules of the Brookings Institution. Public policy should be used to address poverty, not to punish perceived immorality.

There are two ways to address poverty: policy-makers can try either to change people so that they make different choices or to change the world that we live in so that everyone can decide for themselves how to live their lives without the humiliation and deprivation of deep poverty. The decision to change the world is a hard one for middle-class people to accept. It requires everyone to trust one another to make their own decisions, and to acknowledge that there is nothing particularly virtuous about playing by a set of rules that has the effect of helping some of us succeed while others fail. Each one of us knows better than any government bureaucrat, policy-maker, or Brookings Fellow can know what it is we need to make our lives better.

What would happen if we approach one another in a spirit of *radical trust*—a recognition that each one of us knows what it is we need to live better lives? What would our public policy look like? We contend that it would involve a basic income—a guarantee that, no matter what happens in our lives, each one of us has access to enough money to live a modest but dignified life.

References

[1] Jean-Jacques Rousseau, "La 9e Lettre écrite de la montagne" (Paris: Gallimard, 1764), 287.

[2] Jean-Denis Fréchette, "Costing a National Guaranteed Basic Income Using the Ontario Basic Income Model," Office of the Parliamentary Budget Officer, April 18, 2018, https://www.pbo-dpb.gc.ca/web/default/files/Documents/Reports/2018/Basic%20Income/Basic_Income_Costing_EN.pdf

[3] Nasreddine Ammar, Carleigh Busby, and Salma Mohamed Ahmed, "Distributional and Fiscal Analysis of a National Guaranteed Basic Income," Office of the Parliamentary Budget Officer, April 7, 2021. https://www.pbo-dpb.gc.ca/en/blog/news/RP-2122-001-S--distributional-fiscal-analysis-national-guaranteed-basic-income--analyse-financiere-distributive-un-revenu-base-garanti-echelle-nationale

[4] Ron Haskins, "Three Simple Rules Poor Teens Should Follow to Join the Middle Class," The Brookings Institution, 2013, https://www.brookings.edu/opinions/three-simple-rules-poor-teens-should-follow-to-join-the-middle-class/

[5] Marni Brownell, Mariette Chartier, Wendy Au, Leonard MacWilliam, Jennifer Schultz, Wendy Guenette, and Jeff Valdivia, *The Educational Outcomes of Children in Care in Manitoba* (Winnipeg: Manitoba Centre for Health Policy, June 2015), http://mchp-appserv.cpe.umanitoba.ca/reference/CIC_report_web.pdf

[6] Ibid.

[7] Marni Brownell, Nathan Nickel, Lorna Turnbull, Wendy Au, Okechukwu Ekuma, Leonard MacWilliam, Scott McCulloch, Jeff Valdivia, Janelle Boram Lee, Elizabeth Wall-Wieler, and Jennifer Enns, *The Overlap*

between the *Child Welfare and Youth Criminal Justice Systems: Documenting "Cross-Over Kids" in Manitoba* (Winnipeg: Manitoba Centre for Health Policy, 2020), http://mchp-appserv.cpe.umanitoba.ca/reference/MCHP_JustCare_Report_web.pdf

[8] Cindy Blackstock, "Residential Schools: Did They Really Close or Just Morph into Child Welfare?" *Indigenous Law Journal* 6 (2007): 71.

[9] Canadian Press, "The Millennium Scoop: Native Children in Care Surpass Residential School Era," *McGill Newsroom*, August 31, 2011, https://www.mcgill.ca/newsroom/channels/news/canadian-press-millenium-scoop-native-children-care-surpass-residential-school-era-176814

[10] Cindy Blackstock, "The Canadian Human Rights Tribunal on First Nations Child Welfare: Why if Canada Wins, Equality and Justice Lose," *Children and Youth Services Review* 33, no. 1 (2011): 187–94.

[11] National Inquiry into Missing and Murdered Indigenous Women and Girls, *Reclaiming Power and Place: The Final Report of the National Inquiry into Missing and Murdered Indigenous Women and Girls,* vol. 1a, 2019, https://www.mmiwg-ffada.ca/wp-content/uploads/2019/06/Final_Report_Vol_1a-1.pdf

[12] Organization for Economic Co-Operation and Development, "Average Annual Hours Actually Worked per Worker," November 13, 2020, https://stats.oecd.org/Index.aspx?DataSetCode=ANHRS

[13] David Francis, "Why High Earners Work Longer Hours," National Bureau of Economic Research, July 7, 2006, doi: https://www.nber.org/digest/jul06/w11895.html#:~:text=After%20testing%20various%20possible%20causes,for%20the%20%22extra%22%20hours

[14] United Nations, *Universal Declaration of Human Rights*, 1948, https://www.un.org/en/universal-declaration-human-rights/#:~:text=The%20Universal%20Declaration%20of%20Human%20Rights%20(UDHR)%20is%20a%20milestone,the%20history%20of%20human%20rights.&text=It%20sets%20out%2C%20for%20the,translated%20into%20over%20500%20languages

2

Leaving Foster Care for Life as an Adult

On her 18th birthday six years ago, Hailey Cohen was dropped off in front of her high school at Garden City Collegiate in Winnipeg, carrying everything she owned in garbage bags and a few suitcases. Cohen had just moved out of the foster home where she had spent the past five years, and she had nowhere to go. Child and Family Services (CFS) had been a part of her life before she was even born.

"I was dropped off in front of my school and went to my [biological] mom, who was still addicted to drugs. I got right back to the place where I was taken away from," says Cohen, now 24. "It was a huge cycle, [CFS] just put me right back to the beginning. I had nothing, and no knowledge of what to do."

Cohen's story is not unlike the experience of many who transition out of foster care in Manitoba every year. Each province and territory is responsible for ensuring the safety and well-being of children residing in that province, and services are provided across the country under slightly different legislation and administrative processes. According to a CBC News report, at the end of March 2020, 9,849 Manitoba children were in care, of whom 70 per cent were permanent wards. This represented a 4 per cent decline from the previous year. It was still the highest rate of any province. Ninety per cent of

Manitoba children in care were Indigenous, although Indigenous people represent only 18 per cent of the population.[1]

Manitoba's child welfare system has long been criticized for its inability to properly support youth in its care. Former foster kids face high rates of unemployment, housing instability, exploitation, and run-ins with the justice system.[2] According to a 2015 report by the Manitoba Centre for Health Policy, only 33.4 per cent of kids in care graduate high school, compared with 89.3 per cent of students who were never in CFS care.[3]

More than 80 per cent of sexually exploited youth in Manitoba are currently involved with CFS, and 96 per cent are girls and 89 per cent are Indigenous, according to a special report by the Manitoba Advocate for Children and Youth.[4]

The 2018 Winnipeg Street Census reported that of those experiencing homelessness in Winnipeg, half had had some involvement in the child welfare system. Moreover, 62 per cent first experienced homelessness within one year of leaving care.[5]

Preparing Foster Children for Life as Adults

Manitoba CFS is primarily responsible for children under the age of 18, but when children reach that age, they are especially vulnerable. For the first time, a child who may have grown up in foster homes or group homes must navigate the challenges of adult life, figuring out how to budget, how to rent an apartment, where to buy food and how to cook it, and how to find work or continue their schooling.

Between 2017 and 2018, 244 youth aged out of care; of those, 116 were permanent wards, according to documents obtained through the Freedom of Information and Protection of Privacy Act (FIPPA). Child and Family Services will deem a child a "permanent ward" if the child's birth parents have consented to an adoption plan, or if a court of law has determined that parents are unable to care of their child.

It is the responsibility of the child's case manager to ensure all youth have a detailed transition plan for leaving care, according to Manitoba's Child and Family Services Standards Manual.[6] Although transition plans are not entrenched in legislation, the manual suggests starting this process when a youth turns 15. A transition plan could include referrals to needed services like mental health counselling, safe and secure housing, and post-secondary options. All transition plans should be in consultation with the youth and other care providers, family members, or educators.

In addition to having a transition plan, youth aging out may qualify for supports beyond termination of guardianship, also known as "extensions of care." According to section 50, subsection 2 of the Child and Family Services Amendment and Consequential Amendments Act, "The director, or an agency with the written approval of the director, may continue to provide care and maintenance for a former permanent ward for the purpose of assisting the ward to complete the transition to independence, but not beyond the date when the former permanent ward attains the age of 21 years."[7]

In simpler terms, extensions of care are financial supports offered to youth that extend until age 21 in Manitoba.[8] Only kids deemed to be permanent wards are eligible, and supports can be reassessed anywhere from every six months to yearly. In order to continue receiving support, young adults must adhere to their transition plan and conditions or they risk losing support, according to FIPPA documents provided by the Manitoba Department of Families. The success of a youth's accepted transition plan is highly contingent on the youth's obtaining some education. Although this is not explicitly stated in the Act, many young adults say they lost their extensions of care if they dropped out, or were unable to continue, post-secondary programs.

Unfortunately, a perpetually underfunded system with overworked caseworkers and clients who are often uncooperative means that many children reach the age of 18 with no plan and no support.

Cohen says she had no exit strategy in place upon voluntarily leaving care at 18 years old. She says she never completed a transition plan, and neither did anyone tell her about the possibility of extensions of care:

> Basically a few weeks or a month before my 18th birthday, they [caseworkers] were kind of asking me, "What do you want to do? Do you want to leave care?" and stuff like that. On my 18th birthday I was like, I am in an abusive home, my social workers don't listen to me, I'm getting the hell out of here. That was my reason, because they only caused trauma in my life, I felt not supported at all. I was like, I need to leave.

Within a month and a half of leaving the system, she had dropped out of school, was experiencing homelessness, was broke, and was struggling with complex traumas from her time in an abusive foster home.

Young adults have varying experiences when leaving care. This is caused by a number of factors: decisions are made at the discretion of caseworkers; the system is complex, policies can be vague, and transition plans are not part of mandatory legislation. These lead to an overall lack of consistency in exit strategies. In some cases, youth may be supported by a number of people including social workers and foster parents and may continue to receive solid social and financial support after care. However, like Cohen, many youth feel abandoned and unprepared once they reach the age of majority. Additionally, social workers might be overworked and struggling with high paperwork demands and heavy caseloads, which prevents them from providing the necessary attention to children and their families.[9]

Cohen says she felt like a burden during her transition out of the system. "It's not fair that just because I turn 18 my needs don't matter as much, and my desire to have an independent life is shut down. It doesn't make sense. It really destines you for failure," she says.

Six months after leaving care, Cohen had nowhere left to turn. Despite her distrust in the system, she decided to reach out to CFS and ask for help. "I guess I just had no other options. As much as I distrusted the system, this was my parent for so long, this is all I ever knew," she says.

In a rare set of circumstances, Cohen was allowed back into the system. She was assigned a new caseworker, whom she corresponded with only via email, and was told to look for a place to live. She says, "I was homeless at the time because I couldn't live with my mom. She didn't even have a bedroom for me anymore. I was just spending every day at coffee shops looking online for housing, not knowing what to search for. They didn't give me advice or instructions at all. I ended up finding a place really quick."

Once she sent over the rental agreement to her new caseworker, she started receiving financial support. Cohen says she received a cheque for about $400 per month, barely enough to cover her share of rent while living with a roommate.

How much money people receive while on an extension of care varies depending on the circumstances of the individual. Extended supports could cover food, rent, and transportation costs, according to the CFS manual; however, this is also at the discretion of the agency or director. People in very similar circumstances often receive quite different levels of support.

"I couldn't afford food or clothing, or toiletries. I was struggling with almost everything, let alone paying for medicine or counselling. I had to be dependent on whoever I was with, which caused a lot of conflicts in my life," says Cohen. During this time, she experienced sporadic homelessness as housing was always temporary.

Then, on her 21st birthday, the cheques stopped. "It was very hard to lose even just the monthly cheque, no matter how small it was, it was a form of consistency in my life. I was always struggling keeping balance and the small cheque became my only sense of familiarity," she says.

Cohen says she wishes she was better prepared when leaving care at both 18 and 21:

> The system is a parent for so many of us and we need to be taught how to successfully take care of ourselves and live independently. I have relied on Google so much to answer my basic needs and I really wish there was some kind of education on available resources for aging out of care.... I wasn't told how to find free resources, how to job search, how to continue my education while I'm back at my mom's home, how to find food banks, how to do anything independently. It was just basically like good luck, and here are the statistics. This was at 18 and 21, both times there was really no set-up of supports.

Local Groups Fill in Gaps Left by System

The inadequacy of supports offered through CFS has created a need that various advocacy groups and non-profit organizations struggle to fill. Fearless R2W—Circle of Support is a CFS parent advocacy group co-founded by Michael Redhead Champagne and "supergranny" Mary Lund Burton. Champagne is a community organizer and public speaker based in Winnipeg, and Burton is a community and youth support worker who successfully fought the system to gain custody of her grandkids, who were in care. The "R2W" is a postal code in Winnipeg's North End. This postal code has a disconcerting rate of child apprehension, with one in six children in the neighbourhood in the care of child welfare in 2016. The group meets weekly and provides space for parents and youth to learn about Manitoba's welfare system and educate themselves on their rights.

"A lot of the advocates in Fearless are also youth that have aged out themselves, which makes it pretty awesome to have youth that have aged out of care calling out social workers to make sure they give the right supports to families," says Champagne.

In addition to supporting and advocating on behalf of families dealing with child welfare, one issue the group is focused on is eradicating housing instability and homelessness for Indigenous youth transitioning out of care in Winnipeg. The project, titled "Housing Solutions for Indigenous Youth Aging Out of Care in Winnipeg (Housing Solutions WPG)," has also partnered with health researchers at the University of Manitoba, urban planners at HTFC Planning & Design, social innovation consultants, and a collective of youth researchers, some of which are youth in care, called Nigaanii Wabiski Mikanak Ogichidaa (Leading White Turtle Warriors).

"It's been really awesome because we're bringing people from different systems and sectors together so that we can have information from front-line CFS workers, from youth that aged out of care, from youth that are currently aging out of care today," says Champagne.

The project has identified fourteen solutions for better transitioning of youth out of the system. Among the immediate solutions are a residential transition house, coordinated access to social housing, and a kinship support initiative, which would provide youth aging out of care with informal family-type support from community members as they secure and maintain housing.[10]

In 2013, a collaboration originally called Building Futures, now called Futures Forward, was developed through the General Authority of Child and Family Services in partnership with three non-profit organizations: Canadian Mental Health Association Manitoba and Winnipeg, Youth Employment Services Manitoba, and Community Financial Counselling Services. This Manitoba-based collaborative provides wrap-around services to youth in or from Child and Family Services care in Manitoba. The collaborative offers a range of services and support including housing supports, mental health counselling, career and education planning, financial counselling, and system navigation, among others. Services are available to youth aged 15 to 29, and are designed to help youth with the transition into independence.

"There are a lot of agencies who offer one particular service to help, but it can be hard for people to first of all find those resources and that specific access point, but there are still some gaps happening. Our programming having these multiple touch points is working toward seeing less people fall through the cracks," explains Charity Leonard, former executive director of Youth Employment Services Manitoba, one of the Futures Forward collaborative's agency partners.

Leonard says one of the biggest barriers youth face when leaving care is the lack of a social network:

> Social workers help a lot of people while they're still in care, like handling payments or doctor's appointments, but when you no longer have a social worker or have aged out, even knowing necessarily where to find [supports], or how to go advocate for yourself, or even knowing what you're necessarily entitled to, is tough. Often those things are interconnected, so a lack of one thing leads to a lack of another.

According to the CFS manual, in preparing youth to leave care, case managers are responsible for ensuring youth have developed a stable support network.[11] However, Leonard points out that many youths don't have any social supports that they can fall back on. Leonard thinks youth either are not prepared to support themselves when leaving care, or they don't feel prepared enough. However, any young adult leaving home for the first time faces some degree of uncertainty. "A lot of people turning 18 aren't necessarily prepared to just go out on their own," Leonard says. "I know that when I was 18, I still had my parents to fall back on for anything, and I went out there every weekend and I knew that I could do that. A lot of people don't have that luxury. It's hard to be prepared at all at 18, never mind if you've had a lot of instability and a lot of potential trauma."

How Could Basic Income Help?

Advocates argue that basic income, along with other supports like those offered though Futures Forward and Fearless R2W, could provide youth aging out of care with stability and a better sense of independence, and could also help create more consistency in the experiences of youth leaving care. However, some critics argue that a basic income might facilitate poor choices and leave recipients worse off than the current system. Unconditional money might encourage substance use, they say, and encourage young people to be idle rather than search for the kind of stable job that would allow them to thrive.

But those who work in the system and those who have lived with its inadequacies express few concerns about having a basic income. "If I could give the young people [I work with] a basic income I 100 per cent would because when they are empowered financially to make their own decisions, they make great ones," says Champagne.

Cohen says if she were to receive a basic income, it would not only improve her quality of life now, it would have given her more options and security during her transition out of care:

> For basic income ... it should be enough to support a modest life. I think that would be really helpful because that is the core of my struggles right now. I had to stay in an abusive relationship just because it was a source of housing for me. I had to struggle with homelessness because of the lack of financial support there was for me. I know without that stress I would have been way more successful. I would have been thriving, not just surviving.

Cohen moved to Vancouver soon after her 21st birthday on a promise of housing and a fresh start. Once there, she discovered she did not have a place to stay. She says she couch surfed, and was involved in the survival sex industry. "It's just a frustrating thing to look back on because all of these things are a pattern from losing the [cheques]," she says.

Cohen says having a consistent and sufficient income would also have supported her in finding stable work: "If you're focusing on where you're getting your next meal, how are you going to successfully thrive in a work environment? For me, you need stability to be able to work and be able to financially support yourself."

Basic income would have allowed access to a different path. "It is because of my lack of money that I'm going to substance abuse because it's my way of coping with my homelessness, with my lack of food, with my lack of housing, with my lack of schooling. That was my way of coping with all of that. I think that having that financial stability, I wouldn't have been in a situation where I was addicted to drugs," she says.

It took Cohen several years before finding stability in her life. She is now attending Langara College in Vancouver, where she was able to take advantage of British Colombia's tuition waiver program, a bursary given to full-time students with former involvement with child and family services programs.

"It's been three years since I aged out of care. I'm currently in therapy, I attend meetings for my substance abuse, and I'm a full-time student. This is the most years I've lived in the same place since I turned 18," she says. "It's just a really huge accomplishment for me to be doing all of these things and reaching out for help, like trusting a counsellor. I'm still struggling, I'm still going through my trauma, but I feel like I'm finding my footing, finally."

Provinces and Child Welfare Reform

In 2017, Manitoba's Department of Families minister announced a formal review of the province's child welfare legislation. A report by the Legislative Review Committee, published the following year, recommended changes to the CFS system to improve the outcomes of children and youth. Among the recommendations were steps to better support youth transitioning out of care.[12]

The committee proposed that: transition planning for youth in care should be entrenched in the legislation; youth aging out should have priority access to services they need; financial supports should be extended to age 25; and youth should have direct and meaningful input into planning their futures.[13]

On January 1, 2019, the federal government enacted Bill C-92, which gives Indigenous people jurisdiction over child welfare in their communities. The Government of Manitoba announced at the end of 2019 that there would be sweeping reform of Manitoba's Child Welfare Act and that all recommendations from the Legislative Review Committee would be implemented.[14] At the time of writing, no changes have been made.

There is a push from other provinces to extend the age of care so youth can receive supports for longer. British Columbia has extended support for former youth in care to age 21. Groups such as 25 not 21 in Manitoba are pressuring the Manitoba government to follow suit. Yet there are still challenges, and austerity mindsets focus on the direct cost of providing care without recognizing the personal and social costs associated with a lifetime of poverty for those who struggle with the transition out of care. Alberta recently announced that it would eliminate extended care for those aged 22 and older.

References

[1] "Number of Manitoba Kids in CFS Care Down 4 per cent from Last Year," CBC News, October 1, 2020, https://www.cbc.ca/news/canada/manitoba/cfs-child-welfare-system-manitoba-families-kids-in-care-drops-annual-report-1.5746315

[2] Government of Manitoba, Legislative Review Committee, "Transforming Child Welfare Legislation in Manitoba: Opportunities to Improve Outcomes for Children and Youth," 2018, 5, https://www.gov.mb.ca/fs/child_welfare_reform/pubs/final_report.pdf

[3] Marni Brownell, Mariette Chartier, Wendy Au, Leonard MacWilliam, Jennifer Schultz, Wendy Guenette, and Jeff Valdivia, *The Educational Outcomes of Children in Care in Manitoba* (Winnipeg: Manitoba Centre for Health Policy, June 2015), 54, http://mchp-appserv.cpe.umanitoba.ca/reference/CIC_report_web.pdf

[4] Manitoba Advocate for Children and Youth, *A Place Where It Feels Like Home: The Story of Tina Fontaine*, 2019, 91, https://manitobaadvocate.ca/wp-content/uploads/MACY-Special-Report-March-2019-Tina-Fontaine-FINAL1.pdf

[5] Josh Brandon and Christina Maes Nino, *Winnipeg Street Census 2018: Final Report* (Winnipeg: Social Planning Council of Winnipeg, 2018), 5, http://streetcensuswpg.ca/wp-content/uploads/2018/10/2018_FinalReport_Web.pdf

[6] Government of Manitoba, Child and Family Services, "Preparing Youth for Leaving Care," *CFS Manual*, 2019, sect. 1.1.7, https://gov.mb.ca/fs/cfsmanual/1.1.7.html

[7] Government of Manitoba, The Child and Family Services Amendment and Consequential Amendments Act, 1997, c. 48, https://web2.gov.mb.ca/laws/statutes/1997/c04897e.php#24

[8] Ibid.

[9] Joanne Levasseur, "'Agencies Are Really Struggling': High Caseloads, Lack of Staff and Long Waits for Treatment," CBC News, November 7, 2019, https://www.cbc.ca/news/canada/manitoba/west-region-cfs-caseloads-1.5350172

[10] Darrien Morton, Zoë Mager, and Stacy Barter, *Housing Solutions Lab for Indigenous Youth Aging Out of Care Final Report*, 2021.

[11] Government of Manitoba, Child and Family Services, "Preparing Youth."

[12] Government of Manitoba, Legislative Review Committee, *Transforming Child Welfare Legislation in Manitoba: Opportunities to Improve Outcomes for Children and Youth*, 2018, 25, https://www.gov.mb.ca/fs/child_welfare_reform/pubs/final_report.pdf

[13] Ibid.

[14] Government of Manitoba, Department of Families, *Shared Priorities, Sustainable Progress: A 12-month Action Plan for Manitoba Families*, 2019, 8–9, https://www.gov.mb.ca/fs/pubs/shared-priorities-sustainable-progress.pdf

3

Walking with Bear Clan Patrol: Substance Use and Basic Income

Angela Janeczko, coordinator at Bear Clan Patrol, has been safeguarding the streets of Winnipeg's West Broadway neighbourhood every weekend for more than two years.

People can be found sleeping rough in nooks and crannies of the community's back alleys. Dozens of needles and other drug paraphernalia clutter garbage bins around the block. Those people most impacted by addiction are left to fend for themselves, on the street.

Janeczko has personal relationships with those experiencing homelessness and addiction in her community. Addressing them by name, she and her Bear Clan Patrol team hand out soup, sandwiches, granola bars, socks, and mitts.

"In the West Broadway area, we have a huge group of homeless," she says. "It's really about building that relationship and that trust. Now they come looking for us if they're hungry on a Friday, Saturday, or Sunday night."

This work is personal to her; she knows first-hand the struggles of substance use and homelessness.

Janeczko began using drugs after a series of traumas led her to a life of transiency. She and her four children left an abusive relationship in the late 1990s. After losing the financial support from her ex-husband, she relied on Employment and Income Assistance (EIA). "I was a single mother of four with two special-needs children. My children at that time ranged from 7 years old to 6 months old. I was trying to manage it on my own," she says. "I was attempting to pay for a house that was big enough for all of us to live in. My ex-husband became a really psycho-stalker and I still have a restraining order against him to this day."

Not long after, Child and Family Services (CFS) apprehended her four children. "My ex-husband found out that I was moving back home with the kids, and he just told CFS all kinds of lies. They believed them without an investigation. When I lost my kids, it sent me over the edge."

Janeczko says cocaine numbed her pain. "It was doing a line at a party one night and thinking, oh, this isn't too bad. Well, then I wasn't getting high anymore from doing lines, so we were smoking it. Then I wasn't getting high anymore and someone said you can shoot it. I was like, okay, let's try that. Six months into shooting it up, I had sold everything I owned. I was on the street."

Janeczko was homeless for six months while struggling with addiction. "Every penny I had, it would go to drugs. I would do drugs before I paid my rent. I wasn't responsible at all and that's how I ended up being homeless. Then, it was a matter of couch surfing for a while. My friends all got sick of me because I was stealing from them, so they basically threw me out. I survived on the streets until I finally called my mom and said I wanted to come home."

Today, Janeczko shares her lived experience in the hopes of helping others going through the same things. "I just know their struggle. I lived it," she says. "Reliving and telling the story, it's taken a mental toll on me. It's something that's 20 years in my past, and to bring it up, it's been kind of a roller coaster. It's difficult at times and it's helpful at times."

How Does Poverty Fit into the Story?

Janeczko's story shows how the stress of poverty and the indignity of trying to survive with too little can pave the way to substance use.

Rick Lees, former executive director of Main Street Project (MSP), an organization serving people experiencing homelessness in Winnipeg, says the shelter is at capacity every night, and the organization's outreach van patrol serves an additional sixty to one hundred people per night. Many are struggling with substance use. Main Street Project operates a low-barrier facility, meaning people can be using drugs or alcohol and still access services.

Lees notes that not all his clients were experiencing poverty before they began using substances. "We see lots of people who I would say are extremely wealthy or middle class but addiction has stripped them of everything and they have become impoverished. We also have people who are generational; they come from poverty," he says. According to the 2018 Winnipeg Street Census, participants reported addiction or substance use as the second most common factor for first experiencing homelessness (family breakdown was given as most common factor).[1] Addiction is complex, and the experience transcends social and economic status.

There is a close relationship between poverty and addiction, says Jean Doucha, executive director of the Behavioural Health Foundation (BHF), a non-profit addiction and mental health treatment facility in Winnipeg. "Poverty begets addiction in many ways because of the hopelessness of poverty. Addiction becomes a way to cope with the hopelessness of poverty. But the addiction creates poverty as well," Doucha explains.

However, the risks and consequences of substance use vary dramatically by income level. Lees tells the story of a close friend to demonstrate how addiction can play out for someone who begins with greater resources:

He has a good job, a good pension, and his job is such that he can hide it. But when I see him intoxicated, he is no different from the people I've dealt with [at Main Street Project]. He has the same disease; he has the same mental health issues and it'll kill him one way or another.... He can hide it because he earns a big income and he's in a job where he can work from home. I say to him constantly: you are no different in your behaviours and your outcomes from someone living on the street. The journey is similar for ones with money and ones without, but the events that happen aren't the same.

His perception is supported by the data. A recent report by the British Columbia Coroners Service investigated illicit drug overdose deaths between 2016 and 2017 in British Columbia. The study found that 81 per cent of overdose victims were men and the majority of deaths occurred in private homes. Forty-four per cent of people were employed at the time of their death, with over half working in trades and transport.[2] A Statistics Canada report shows that in 2018, the average hourly wage for a full-time employee in trades, transport, equipment operation, and related occupations in Canada was $26 per hour, and about $41 per hour for people working in middle-management positions.[3] These figures show that addiction can impact people from all backgrounds and socio-economic classes. Where money does make a difference, though, is along the path to recovery.

In *Drugging the Poor*, author Merrill Singer states that while drugs may impact people from all socio-economic backgrounds, the effects of addiction are much worse in low-income communities: "While drug use occurs in all strata in ... society, the effects of drug use are not equally distributed. Drug use accounts for some of the morbidity and mortality in the upper social classes—with alcoholism and tobacco-related illnesses taking the greatest toll; among the poor, however, it is a significant source of sickness, suffering, and death."[4]

Addiction is perceived differently, depending on social standing. According to Singer, "Inner-city illicit drug use and sales have come to be synonymous with lack of control, senseless violence, and moral decay. Drug addicts as a group … have become pretty much worthless humans in the popular imagination."[5]

Janeczko agrees that this flawed perception persists. She says the lack of dignity was one of the biggest barriers she faced while experiencing homelessness. "It's a fight for dignity, it's the fight to just stay alive," she says. "I've had feces thrown at me for being out on the street, I've been spit on, I've been called a bum. There's this stigma: if you're on the street you're portrayed as being a loser, you're not worth anything. That's how our government looks at us. We're just a number."

Doucha emphasizes that it is much more difficult for those living in poverty to get addictions support than those who are more affluent. "Is addiction harder for people who are impoverished? Absolutely. I think that withdrawal is going to be the same no matter who you are. But the roadmap that you find yourself on to get to that point of finally needing to withdraw is going to be very different," says Doucha. "You can be coddled through it as a person of affluence. You can't be coddled through it as a person who doesn't have a pot to piss in, and that's really sad to watch."

The Behavioural Health Foundation (BHF) and other publicly funded addictions treatment centres in the province of Manitoba have long wait-lists for services, says Doucha. "Sadly, we have over ninety people waiting for a bed at BHF. It's been the norm for the past five years to have high waiting lists. Manitoba does have a lot of treatment providers but we all face huge wait-lists. People need help for immediate services but we can't provide it."

Between 2018 and 2019, there were 368 residents who came through BHF's addiction treatment facility. The centre has co-ed, family, and women-only facilities and houses 114 treatment beds in total.[6] Addictions Foundation of Manitoba (AFM) provides publicly funded in-house and community-based addiction treatment services across the province. Between 2018 and 2019, there were 2,280 patients in in-house treatment and 16,120 clients who sought community-based treatment. The majority of AFM's clients have a median annual income of $29,999 or lower.

There are also several public addictions treatment centres run by religion-based organizations in Manitoba. Some people choose not to access these services because they feel uncomfortable seeking treatment in faith-based environments, says Lees. Additionally, there are privately run addiction facilities in the province; Aurora Recovery Centre is one of them. Located in Gimli, Manitoba, the facility runs thirty- to ninety-day detoxing and addictions treatment programs. The minimum thirty-day program costs $19,900. Most people stay for the forty-five-day program at a cost of nearly $27,000. There is currently no wait-list for services.[7]

Lees says the structure of privately funded treatment creates classism in addiction. "To be honest, if they were going to treat addiction as an even playing field, [private facilities] would accept anyone, but they're not. They're going to accept people who can pay. This contributes to the idea that addiction is class related and that certain classes deserve treatment. That is frustrating because the constituents I've worked with have no access to [private] facilities, and they need the help."

"Won't Giving Money to People Who Use Drugs Harm Them?"

One of the most common criticisms of basic income is rooted in an assumption that people will just use it to fund their habit, making their lives and the lives of their families worse in the process.

Janeczko fears that money can be a trigger for drug use:

> You got money? First place you go is to your drug dealer. It's an absolute trigger. At some point, you lose control of your ability to function and your life becomes the need for the drug and you find any way to get those drugs.... I don't think a basic income would make much difference for users. If they're not at the point where they want to get clean or become productive in society, money won't make a difference because they still have it in their minds that drugs are most important. For addicts, drugs are more important than food, than clothes, it's more important than anything.

However, evidence from cash-transfer experiments showed a much more hopeful outcome. A 2020 study funded by the Vancouver-based organization Foundations for Social Change was designed to determine how a direct cash transfer might impact the lives of those experiencing homelessness in British Columbia. Fifty individuals were chosen to receive a one-time cash payment of $7,500, which was deposited in one lump sum into participants' bank accounts. Participants were selected based on age, length of time experiencing homelessness, degree of mental health, and severity of substance and alcohol use. Although this study wasn't specifically designed for people using drugs or alcohol, results show reduced spending on drugs, cigarettes, and alcohol, among other findings.[8]

> Over 12 months, cash recipients reduced spending [by 39 per cent] on goods such as alcohol, cigarettes, or drugs. There is a widespread misperception that people in poverty will spend money they receive on goods such as alcohol, cigarettes, or drugs. This finding challenges such misperception, demonstrating that participants reduce their spending on temptation goods after receiving cash transfers.... Most spending was devoted to rent, food, and other recurring

expenditures like bills. Some cash participants also used the money to purchase food and clothing for their children. Cash transfers provided choice and enabled people to buy more goods, helping them meet their basic needs.[9]

Similarly, a study in Liberia gave cash and behavioural therapy to at-risk young men who were undereducated, living in poverty, and susceptible to violence, and had a pre-existing addiction to drugs. Researchers wanted to know the effects of giving these men therapy or cash, or both. Much like in the cash-transfer project in British Columbia, cash payments were primarily spent on basic needs. Recipients reported spending the grant on food and shelter and business investments, and some recipients saved earnings and made debt payments. Regardless of therapy, little of the grant was spent on drugs.[10]

Lees believes a basic income would not increase drug use:

> We need to have a basic income because income is never proven to be the issue around addiction, in my opinion.... I don't see a basic income increasing drug use. The difference is that it would stabilize things. Withdrawal is a terrible thing and people can die from it, so absolutely if someone is getting any money from either panhandling or from EIA, first they'll spend it on drugs. Our system forces people to cycle from nothing to something.

Doucha says people will use drugs no matter their income, but a basic income would allow them more autonomy and choice over their lives: "Some people are going to use some of that money to get high. They may blow their allowance this year or this month, but maybe next month that will change for them. Right now, society isn't meeting people's basic needs and I think that has got to be the priority."

Basic Income as a Harm-Reduction Strategy

A basic income would provide people who are using drugs a little bit of dignity. Instead of sleeping rough or spending the night on a mat at a crowded shelter, they would have options for something better. Moreover, people who use drugs may be less reliant on committing petty crimes in order to feed their addiction.

A basic income has never been proven to increase drug or alcohol use. People will use drugs no matter their income. However, a basic income would also allow people to choose their own road to recovery.

Janeczko spent six months living on the street while addicted to cocaine. It wasn't until a close friend of hers died that she realized she was heading down a dangerous path: "I don't think it really registered in my mind that [cocaine] could kill me. When I heard that Chad died, it was 'oh my god, this is real.' Chad was my best friend, who still is my best friend. It was very personal, and it hurt really bad. From the day I heard he died, that was it for me."

Within the addictions treatment sector, one of the most interesting and productive paths that have emerged in recent years is that of harm reduction, which refers to interventions meant to reduce or eliminate unhealthy outcomes from continued engagement in high-risk behaviours. Harm reduction explicitly recognizes the ability of substance users to take control of their own lives.

For example, controlled or moderate drinking is an alternative treatment to sobriety for some people who are alcohol-dependent. A shelter in Ottawa began the Moderate Alcohol Program (MAP) with the intent to stabilize people's dependency on alcohol. At The Oaks, clients receive a medically prescribed dosage of wine every hour for fifteen hours per day. This structured consumption has significantly reduced the amount of alcohol consumed at one time and helped clients remain stable in order to address their addiction. Overall, alcohol consumption was reduced significantly for some participants and others even refrained from consumption entirely.[11]

When it comes to abstinence from drugs, the same harm-reduction methods may apply. Drug use in controlled spaces, like safe injection sites, may limit the risks of binging or other harmful behaviours associated with drug use. According to a study from the UK, most drug users who sought abstinence treatment weren't able to maintain sobriety after completing the programs.[12]

Doucha says that while they are in BHF treatment, people are expected to abstain from substances. However, she understands that might not be a long-term solution for everyone. "Our goal is to get them healthy again so they can make better decisions for themselves. Our goal is not abstinence for every person; we don't think that's realistic. Most people who do treatment return to some drug use, whether that be alcohol or other drugs. We don't think that's a bad thing," she says.

This aligns with the goals of basic income, which are based in the assumption that everyone is entitled to, and has the capacity to, make their own decisions.

Janeczko says a basic income would make a big difference in the lives of those in, or seeking, treatment: "At the point where they want to get help or are in treatment, I think it would be very helpful. They could get housing, they could get furniture, they could get their basic needs met. That way they could start building a life for themselves. If they are constantly struggling to find money and it's not there, they're going to revert back to the old," she says.

A basic income would allow people who use drugs and alcohol more autonomy over their lives, says Doucha: "In time it becomes that the addiction is not even the central issue anymore. It's the other things. It is the fact that you're still facing poverty, they don't have a good job lined up, they don't have a decent place to live, and they don't have a support system in the community because they burned all their bridges. Those are the primary concerns for people with addiction issues."

Lees says a basic income would give people who use drugs the ability to meet their basic needs, which may include keeping their withdrawal at bay:

> We had a guy who we paid under the table at Mainstay [supportive transitional housing at MSP] doing janitorial work and he wanted a bit more money but if we put him on our payroll, he would be cut off from EIA. So, literally we would pay him cash. We had to get around the system. He had a little extra money and he didn't use any more of it than he already used on drugs, but he ate a little better, he dressed a little better and he had a better sense of self-worth.

Our society collectively treats people who use drugs as undeserving. No one is undeserving; and a basic income is not something you need to deserve or earn—it's a right. It offers recipients the opportunity and freedom to live another kind of life if they choose to do so. In many ways it's like harm-reduction programs; we don't mandate sobriety. Basic income gives everyone the opportunity to make their lives a little better; when people have real choice, they have more opportunity to control their own behaviours and responses.

References

[1] Josh Brandon and Christina Maes Nino, *Winnipeg Street Census 2018: Final Report* (Winnipeg: Social Planning Council of Winnipeg, 2018), 5, http://streetcensuswpg.ca/wp-content/uploads/2018/10/2018_FinalReport_Web.pdf

[2] Ministry of Public Safety and Solicitor General, Coroners Service, *Illicit Drug Overdose Deaths in BC: Findings of Coroners' Investigations,* 2018, 5, https://www2.gov.bc.ca/assets/gov/birth-adoption-death-marriage-and-divorce/deaths/coroners-service/statistical/illicitdrugoverdosedeathsinbc-findingsofcoronersinvestigations-final.pdf

[3] Statistics Canada, *Employee Wages by Occupation, Annual, Inactive,* 2018, https://www150.statcan.gc.ca/t1/tbl1/en/tv.action?pid=1410030701

[4] Merrill Singer, *Drugging the Poor: Legal and Illegal Drugs and Social Inequality* (Long Grove, IL: Waveland Press, 2018), 18.

[5] Ibid., 232.

[6] Behavorial Health Foundation, *Annual Report April 1, 2018–March 31, 2019,* 4.

[7] Aurora Recovery Centre. Treatment services and prices were provided by the facility.

[8] Foundations for Social Change: New Leaf Project, *Taking Bold Action on Homelessness*, 2020, 3, https://static1.squarespace.com/static/5f07a92f21d34b403c788e05/t/5f751297fcfe7968a6a9 57a8/1601507995038/2020_09_30_FSC_Statement_of_Impact_w_ Expansion.pdf

[9] ibid., 12–15.

[10] Christopher Blattman, Julian C. Jamison, and Margaret Sheridan, "Reducing Crime and Violence: Experimental Evidence from Cognitive Behavioral Therapy in Liberia," *American Economic Review* 107, no. 4 (April 2017): 1168–1187, https://www.poverty-action.org/sites/default/files/publications/1007_CBT-Liberia-AER-Apr2017.pdf

[11] The Oaks, *Shepherds of Good Hope*, n.d., https://www.sghottawa.com/the_oaks/

[12] Neil Mckeganey, Zoë Morris, Jo Neale, and Michele Robertson, "What Are Drug Users Looking for When They Contact Drug Services: Abstinence or Harm Reduction?" *Drugs: Education, Prevention and Policy* 11, no. 5 (October 2004): 431, https://www.researchgate.net/profile/Neil_Mckeganey/publication/40710392_What_are_drug_users_looking_for_when_they_contact_drug_services_Abstinence_or_harm_reduction/links/0c96051545661713e5000000/What-are-drug-users-looking-for-when-they-contact-drug-services-Abstinence-or-harm-reduction.pdf

4

Life After Prison

After nearly fifteen years spent in the revolving door of the justice system in Manitoba, Vinnie Lillie decided to start his life over. In February 2012, Lillie completed his last stint at Stony Mountain Institution and walked away from prison for good. "I wish I would have started earlier looking at how good my life is now," he says. Making this decision meant leaving behind everything he knew: crime, gang life, addiction, and the routine of incarceration.

Leaving Incarceration Can Be Stressful
Lillie says leaving the justice system in Manitoba was a tough transition. The lack of support on the outside led him into a vicious cycle of reoffending, breaching parole, and going back to prison: "I was definitely institutionalized because when I got out on the street I would never last, maybe a couple months," he says. "Most people would be sad or mad that they were going back to jail, but I was happy because I was going back to what I knew and I didn't have to worry about what tomorrow would bring."

Many people transitioning out of the justice system find it hard to reintegrate into society, says Senator Kim Pate, former executive director of the Canadian Association of Elizabeth Frye Societies. She says one of the biggest barriers people face is the lack of resources to be able to support themselves once they're out. This may lead people to reoffend:

> There's three main things people need to be successful when they get out. One, not surprisingly, is the community of support, whether it's family or communities, people who care about them. Second is a place to live and something meaningful to do. Third is a way to support themselves. For many that ends up being social assistance because it's very hard to get a job when you've been in prison. There are huge poverty-related challenges for people getting out and being able to get back on their feet.

Sharon Perrault, the acting executive director of the John Howard Society of Manitoba, says the transition from incarceration is often very stressful:

> When we look at that plan of reintegration going forward, there are so many systems that need to be involved and so many interventions. Self-directed motivation, for some, is often lacking because they've been doing this for a long time and violence becomes normalized.... Then we combine that with their history. They've often had little employment, particularly steady employment, or erratic and sporadic employment. There's always a certain amount of stress related to people coming out and kind of navigating the world.

Lillie says he could have benefited from additional services after he left the justice system: "You get out and the resources just aren't there for you that you need. These people who get out need that support because they don't have money, or a place to live. People go back to what they know so easily."

Drawn In by Promise of Belonging

Lillie's first run-in with the justice system was when he was only 14 years old. He got caught up with the wrong crowd in his early teens, dropped out of school, and spent his days hanging around 7-Eleven, smoking and selling weed. It wasn't long before he was initiated into a gang.

"I was just looking for something that I was missing. These people that I got involved with who are part of the gangs gave me what I was looking for: the attention," says Lillie. "I was really just embracing being embraced by other people."

Lillie was the youngest of four boys and lived with his mom in Winnipeg's North End. His father left when he was only 3. "I don't even remember much of my childhood because I blocked most of it out. The housing situation I lived in as a kid was a party house, drug dealers and loud music every night. I just think about how many traumas I went through as a kid. I don't remember shit, I don't remember birthdays, I don't remember Christmas, I don't remember nothing. I didn't know I was sexually abused until I was 30."

Lillie says the lack of attention and care he received as a kid made gang life enticing. "I find that it's not just me but a lot of people are attracted to that type of lifestyle. That's why people get involved in organized crime because it's the money, the women, the drugs, the fast life. It draws people in. For me, I got that feeling for sure," he says.

At 21, Lillie was serving his first sentence in prison for armed robbery. By the time he was in his mid-30s, he had spent a total of nine years behind bars. "When I became an adult, I got involved in the harder drugs, like cocaine. That's when I started learning from people around me about doing robberies. So, basically that's what I would do. I was involved in doing crack and robbing convenience stores. All my convictions are from robberies," he says.

Volunteering Creates Purpose—But Not Income

Lillie says a lot of self-reflection and counselling went into his decision to leave gang and crime life behind: "I realized that what I was doing was using anger as my fuel to keep doing the things that I was doing."

He's now a dedicated volunteer and works to tell his story to community groups and in schools across Winnipeg in the hope that his message will prevent at-risk youth from getting involved in gangs. He's also a member of Ogijiita Pimatiswin Kinamatwin (OPK), which supports men who are involved in gangs or the justice system. Volunteer work is his passion and what drives him. He became emotional when he talked about being able to deliver more than 200 Christmas hampers to Winnipeggers in need. However, he doesn't make an income from the hours of work he does in the community. As a result, Lillie is living on Employment and Income Assistance (EIA) to make ends meet.

EIA has been criticized for providing insufficient income that barely covers basic needs and costs of living, but there are additional issues for people with involvement in the justice system. The Outstanding Warrant Policy may prevent people from accessing EIA if they have an outstanding warrant for a serious crime.[1] For someone who is already collecting EIA, they may be cut off from support if there is a warrant out for their arrest. Warrants can be issued for a variety of reasons, including to ensure a defendant appears in court or to prevent a repeat offence.[2] Warrants may also be issued if someone breaches conditions of their parole or probation. This could be as simple as missing a meeting with a probation or parole officer.

The Canadian Centre for Policy Alternatives Manitoba Office released a statement in 2012 that criticized the Outstanding Warrant Policy for criminalizing people living in poverty: "In effect, the [policy] will turn the EIA program from a system of protection to one of punishment and enforcement, fundamentally changing its purpose, scope and performance."[3]

Lillie says he hasn't had the easiest time accessing EIA. His volunteer work is most important to him; however, in order to continue to qualify for social assistance, he has to be job searching and available for work:

> It's made things harder because I don't have anything to fall back on. I'm very blessed that I don't really care about money, but I do need money to survive. I've had a lot of jobs, but they never last. I always got into that cycle of not caring about working. You're not used to working, you've never done a resume or anything like that.... EIA said I had to look for a job and I couldn't just continue to do volunteer work and they couldn't support that.

EIA rules reflect the value society places on paid work over volunteer work. However, volunteering plays crucial roles in society, both by providing direct support to others and by developing life skills in people who may not have the basic skills and attitudes that make them employable in this society. There are many benefits of volunteering, including skills building, community building, citizen engagement, social inclusion, belonging, and enhancing democracy, according to Volunteer Canada.[4]

Finding long-term meaningful work with a criminal record remains a challenge for Lillie. He says he recently started working sixteen hours a week in a group home.

Social Enterprise Offers "Another Path" to Employment

BUILD Inc., co-founded by Shaun Loney, is a social enterprise that hires and trains people who would otherwise struggle to find a job. Applicants are hired when they have a criminal record, no driver's licence, and a lack of work experience.

"BUILD addresses what I believe to be Canada's defining issue—connecting people who most need the work with the work that most needs to be done," says Loney. The organization specializes in energy and water retrofits in Manitoba Housing complexes and employs anywhere from eighty to one hundred people at a time. In fact, there is such a huge demand for employment at BUILD that lineups of people often stretch around the Social Enterprise Centre in Winnipeg's North End, which is the contractor's headquarters.

Loney says this demand stems from the lack of opportunities for people with a criminal record: "What BUILD does is say, well, because you don't have a driver's licence or work experience, we're going to hire you here. They will come to BUILD with sort of a minus $15 wage in the labour market, and they leave at $15 while they're working." More than 75 per cent of incarcerated men in Manitoba reoffend within two years of their release from provincial custody.[5] At BUILD, only 20 per cent of its employees reoffend, says Loney.

"They just keep moving in a more helpful way. They've had access to Elders, they've had access to peer mentors, they've had housing advocacy, and they've become more employable because they have their driver's licence. This kind of opens up a whole new world of possibility," says Loney. "If you come here you get a taste of what that other world looks like. If people believe that you can do it, and you're seeing other people doing it, you see that there is another path besides incarceration."

Perrault says employment could prevent recidivism by creating structure and improving self-esteem. "I firmly believe that when people work, particularly when they're working five days a week, they're too tired to commit a crime. I think a lot of people get involved in criminality because of lack of structure," says Perrault. "Most people don't want to live in a desperate state because it doesn't feel good, they want to be able to have a sense of accomplishment in some way."

The Role of Basic Income

The importance of work, however, doesn't mean there is no role for a basic income. Access to support without a work requirement would help to keep people out of the justice system in the first place and help those who are incarcerated to adjust to society upon their release.

Loney says there is a direct correlation between poverty and crime:

> I think the corrections system fails to recognize why people are committing offences in the first place. Many of these guys will tell you, "I was selling drugs to make some money because I didn't have any other options." Especially if they're too proud to go on social assistance or they're ineligible for social assistance because they are able-bodied men. I think basic income would cause an immediate reduction in crime.

Perrault echoes this sentiment: "I know few people who are in jail who are wealthy; they are all poor. They started off as poor, and it's very difficult to break that pattern of poverty. People who are at the bottom tend to stay there. How do you climb out of that?"

Lillie says a basic income would also provide people with stability and a safety net to help them get back on their feet after incarceration:

> It's like if you had a big huge beautiful tree but it's sick and you want to fix it. What do you do? You go to the root of it and you start at the root. With people getting out of jail, of course there's the concern about what people do with a bunch of money, but when you think about it, money is the root of what their stress is going to come from. They're going to worry about where they're going to sleep, what they're going to eat. When you start with money you give them that comfort level.

He says providing formerly incarcerated people with a safety net will give them a chance to address the reasons why they are drawn into crime in the first place. "Money takes that stress away. If they're not stressed out about where their next meal is coming from, or where they're going to sleep, then they can sit down and process the bigger pieces they need to tackle."

Processing these "bigger pieces" becomes part of finding meaning and purpose. Activist, professor, and scholar Cindy Blackstock says that one of the reasons ideas such as Maslow's Hierarchy, which is informed by Blackfoot beliefs, finds such resonance with many people is because it seems so intuitive.[6] Abraham Maslow suggests that people are motivated first to fulfill basic needs, like shelter, food, and clothing, before they can find meaning in life. Once those basic needs are met, people can move to the need for safety and security and advance to love and intimacy and then self-esteem. The highest level is when people become self-aware and grow to reach their potential. Only after people have their basic needs met do they have the opportunity to think about self-actualization and meaning in life. Basic income has the ability to address these primary needs by providing stability and a sense of financial security.

The Gang Action Interagency Network, or GAIN, is a non-profit coalition of organizations working to prevent gang involvement and raise awareness about gang prevention in Winnipeg. Former coordinator Sean Sousa says a basic income would make a big difference in the lives of those people formerly involved in gangs:

> People say, "I want out of the gang but I don't know how to live." A basic income would at least make you secure and make you stable. Stable enough to rent a house, stable enough to keep you on your feet rather than having to go back to finding income in illegitimate ways. You can figure out what to do next, at least, if you have a basic income. I really want to emphasize that after you exit or are ready to

exit a gang, basic income would be a game changer for a lot of people's life. When you find stability, you can figure out what you're really trying to do. That's very important.

Senator Pate says a basic income would not only help those transitioning out of prison, it may even prevent people from committing crime in the first place:

> I think we'd see fewer people going into the system because of poverty. I think it could help prevent people from being criminalized in the first place. People who have no other means end up criminalized as they try to negotiate poverty. For those who are criminalized and imprisoned, you could certainly assist people to get on their feet much more quickly and allow them to pursue education or vocational training if that's what they need so they can then sustain themselves.

For Lillie, a basic income would allow him to provide more for his three kids: "The main thing is that I want to be able to get things for my kids or to have the money to do stuff with my kids. I don't care about myself, it's them who I care about," he says.

A biography about Lillie's life, entitled *All Eyes on Me*, written by Kevin Zdrill, was released in October of 2020.[7]

Justice Systems Disproportionately Affect Indigenous People

According to the latest Statistics Canada data, there are nearly 24,657 adults in provincial and territorial custody and 14,129 in federal custody. Manitoba has the highest rate of adult incarceration in the country, followed by Saskatchewan and Alberta. Indigenous adults account for 75 per cent of total offenders in Manitoba, although they represent only 18 per cent of the overall population of the province.[8]

A 2020 report by the Correctional Investigator of Canada found that Indigenous people now represent more than 30 per cent of federal inmates in custody across Canada, even though they account for only 5 per cent of the general Canadian population.[9] The report suggests that surpassing this 30 per cent mark indicates a deepening "Indigenization" of the corrections system in Canada.

There is a troubling trend in incarceration rates of women, especially Indigenous women. A book by scholar Shoshana Pollock says that about 80 per cent of women in prison are there because of poverty-related crimes.[10] Convictions for Indigenous women are commonly theft under $5,000, theft over $5,000, fraud, and trafficking drugs, according to the National Inquiry into Missing and Murdered Indigenous Women and Girls.[11]

Statistics Canada indicates that about 80 per cent of incarcerated youth in Manitoba are Indigenous, and nearly half of minors who end up in custody across Canada are Indigenous.[12]

In a ten-day span starting on April 8, 2020, the Winnipeg Police Service shot and killed three Indigenous people. One of the victims was Eishia Hudson, a 16-year-old girl. An investigation into Hudson's death was done by the Independent Investigation Unit of Manitoba, but no charges were recommended against the officer involved.[13] CBC News reported that since 2000, nineteen people have been shot and killed by members of the Winnipeg Police Service. Of those, twelve were Indigenous.[14] Since the 2020 shootings by Winnipeg police, many community leaders have spoken out to demand a substantial defunding of the Winnipeg Police Service's budget and reinvestment in community supports.

Corrections Cost Governments Billions

The average daily cost for keeping just one inmate incarcerated is about $344, or $125,466 per year.[15] The annual cost of keeping a man incarcerated federally is about $121,339 per year, and the annual cost of imprisoning a woman in federal corrections is $212,005.[16] The average annual cost per prisoner in provincial jails is approximately $67,000.[17]

The latest Statistics Canada 2017–18 figures show adult corrections services cost the federal government $5 billion per year,[18] and provincial and territorial governments more than $2.6 billion per year.[19]

References

[1] Government of Canada, Department of Families, "Outstanding Warrant Policy," n.d., https://www.gov.mb.ca/fs/eia/outstanding_warrants.html

[2] Government of Manitoba, The Provincial Offences Act, 2013, 160, https://web2.gov.mb.ca/laws/statutes/ccsm/p160e.php

[3] Canadian Centre for Policy Alternatives Manitoba Office, *Denying EIA Benefits Because of Outstanding Warrants—Unwarranted!,* 2012, http://www.policyalternatives.ca/sites/default/files/uploads/publications/Manitoba%20Office/2012/11/Denying%20EIA.pdf

[4] Volunteer Canada, "Value of Volunteering Wheel," n.d., https://volunteer.ca/index.php?MenuItemID=383

[5] Shaun Loney, *An Army of Problem Solvers* (Winnipeg: Friesens, 2016), 78.

[6] Cindy Blackstock, "The Emergence of the Breath of Life Theory," *Journal of Social Work Values and Ethics* 8, no. 1 (2011), 3-4.

[7] Kevin Zdrill, *All eyes on Me: A True Story of Addiction, Recovery and Hope* (Winnipeg: FriesenPress, 2020), https://friesenpress-accounts.appspot.com/store/title/119734000019711820/Kevin-Zdrill-All-Eyes-On-Me

[8] Statistics Canada, *Adult and Youth Correctional Statistics in Canada, 2017/2018,* 2018, https://www150.statcan.gc.ca/n1/pub/85-002-x/2019001/article/00010-eng.htm

[9] Correctional Investigator of Canada, *Indigenous People in Federal Custody Surpasses 30%,* 2020, https://www.oci-bec.gc.ca/cnt/comm/press/press20200121-eng.aspx, 2020

[10] Shoshana Pollock, *Locked In, Locked Out: Imprisoning Women in the Shrinking and Punitive Welfare State* (Waterloo: Wilfred Laurier University Press, 2008), 6.

[11] National Inquiry into Missing and Murdered Indigenous Women and Girls, *Reclaiming Power and Place: The Final Report of the National Inquiry into Missing and Murdered Indigenous Women and Girls*, Vol. 1a, 2019, 637, https://www.mmiwg-ffada.ca/wp-content/uploads/2019/06/Final_Report_Vol_1a-1.pdf

[12] Statistics Canada, *Adult and Youth Correctional Statistics in Canada, 2016/2017*, 2017, https://www150.statcan.gc.ca/n1/daily-quotidien/180619/dq180619a-eng.htm

[13] Independent Investigation Unit of Manitoba, "Final Report: IIU Concludes Investigation into Fatal WPS Officer-Involved Shooting," January 2021, http://www.iiumanitoba.ca/pdf/final_report_2020-018.pdf

[14] Jacques Marcoux, "After 4 Fatal Police Shootings in 40 Days, Grand Chief Wants Manitoba Officers to Wear Body Cams." CBC News, April 29, 2020, https://www.cbc.ca/news/canada/manitoba/arlen-dumas-police-body-cams-1.5548721

[15] Statistics Canada, *2019 Annual Report: Corrections and Conditional Release Statistical Overview*, 2020, https://www.publicsafety.gc.ca/cnt/rsrcs/pblctns/ccrso-2019/index-en.aspx#b1

[16] Ibid.

[17] The John Howard Society of Canada, "Financial Facts of Canadian Prisons," n.d., https://johnhoward.ca/blog/financial-facts-canadian-prisons/

[18] Statistics Canada, *Adult and Youth Correctional Statistics*, 2018.

[19] Statistics Canada, *2019 Annual Report*.

5

Trapped in the Precariat

One of the benefits of basic income is that it both provides support for those who are not working and supplements the earnings of those in low-paid, precarious work. Societal trends that were already well entrenched before COVID-19 were highlighted, and sometimes accelerated, by the pandemic. Many people with well-paid, professional jobs were sent home to work remotely for the duration and continued to collect a paycheque. Some workers, though, were unable to work from home and continued to perform necessary jobs that required them to put their health and that of their families at risk by going out to work and interacting with the public every day. Some of these front-line workers were essential and relatively well-paid healthcare workers, while others were bus drivers, grocery store cashiers, food delivery and Uber drivers, personal support workers, agricultural workers, and all the many kinds of workers whose labour is essential to daily life but who get little policy attention during ordinary times. There was a brief flurry of public recognition and support for such workers, and temporary wage subsidies for some, but many front-line service providers continued to work in precarious, low-paid jobs throughout the pandemic just as they had before COVID-19.

The pandemic highlighted trends that had been decades in the making. Precarious work had been growing as a proportion of total employment for many years. From the perspective of employers, hiring workers by the hour with no promise of a lifetime job or regular hours creates flexibility that allows them to adapt to changing competitive conditions. Some workers, too, benefit from temporary contracts and part-time work as long as those are a choice and not a necessity. Flexible hours often allow workers the freedom to spend time on education or artistic endeavours, which accounts for the high proportion of minimum-wage workers who are under 25 years old. However, not all workers in precarious employment are there by choice and, for many, it becomes a lifetime trap of low wages and economic insecurity.

Young people, newcomers, racialized people, and women are more likely to be working in low-paid jobs with little security. The factors that account for this are rooted deep in our society, and addressing them requires much more than just income support. Nevertheless, basic income is necessary for two reasons: first, it ensures that everyone has enough to survive so that some people can dedicate their time to creating larger, systemic changes; and, second, it ensures that the heaviest burden of working for systemic change is not imposed on those least able to support it. Change takes time. Some have criticized basic income because it does not challenge precarious and degrading work directly.[1] However, it's hard to accept the morality of forcing people in low-paid precarious work to wait for social change and, in the meantime, to live without the resources to put food on the table and pay the rent. A basic income ensures that the most vulnerable people have the means to live and the time to advocate for social change, rather than lurching from crisis to crisis, constantly searching for paid work or other supports and struggling just to make ends meet.

Racism and Precarious Work
Race is an important barrier to economic equality and well-being. People of colour are more likely to earn low incomes, face

job precarity, and suffer from poverty than white Canadians.[2] According to the 2016 Census, 22.7 per cent of the population are non-white and received incomes that were 74 per cent of those received by white Canadians. This number has remained almost unchanged over the past decade.[3] Basic income cannot address the fundamental challenges posed by race and cultural identity in Canada, but it can offset some of the economic consequences and provide a platform that helps people to pursue opportunities that may have been out of reach. This includes the unpaid, underpaid, and very demanding work of helping to bring about social change.

Josephine Grey is long-time human rights defender, public speaker, and community organizer based in Toronto, Ontario. She says low wages and precarious work have prevented many members of her community from engaging in advocacy work.

Grey has helped found several organizations, including Foodshare Toronto, St. James Town Community Cooperative (SJT Co-op), the Eco-Just Food Network, and the Ontario Basic Income Network. She is also known for reporting to the United Nations on Ontario's violations of economic, social, and cultural rights. Her recent work is with Low Income Families of Toronto (LIFT), an organization she also founded. LIFT works on projects that focus on improving healthy food security and human rights in St. James Town, a multicultural, multilingual, and multi-ethnic high-rise community where newcomers make up a large proportion of the population.[4] According the the St. James Town Service Providers' Network, 61 per cent of St. James Town residents are people of colour.[5] Projects at LIFT are always developed in collaboration with the community, but precarious work and low wages prevent many from participating.

"It's been incredibly difficult to keep our community engaged in [LIFT's] vision because everybody is working a lot of low-wage precarious jobs, and it's very difficult to engage community development these days," Grey says.

St. James Town is Canada's most densely populated neighbourhood, and about 40 per cent of residents live in poverty.[6] Grey says she's frustrated by how the low wage trap prevents people from doing important community work. "People of colour have narrower choice and fewer opportunities. We could be doing a lot more together collaboratively if they [people in St. James Town] had the time, freedom, and resources to do so," she says.

As an immigrant, mixed-race person, and survivor of domestic violence, Grey can relate to the experiences of many people in her community. Grey was born to a white woman raised in Uganda and a Jamaican father she never knew. Racism and discrimination in social systems have been a part of her life since she was born:

> The long-lingering and now increasingly toxic revived effects of white supremacy and racism have been a part of my life, throughout my life. My mother had to move to Canada because I was mixed-race and it wouldn't be safe for me to be in England at the time. My children are even more mixed-race, they include being Indigenous, and the effects on their father's family of the colonial legacy, and then the effects of our reversal of progress around racism, has impacted my family all along, and my neighbourhood. It's a huge part of my experience.... I was observing in a lot of different ways how the system was set up to do good things but in its actually delivery was very screwed up. I was dealing with the income system, I was dealing with the housing system, and I was dealing with the food system. My interactions with social services were often humiliating, triggering, there was discrimination in those systems. So, I became more and more radicalized, shall I say, by my struggles.

Grey says she turned her experiences into fuel to create change. However, much of the work she does is unpaid:

> There have been years where I was able to get grants and get paid for my work, but many years of my career I have not been paid. While I was on Mother's Allowance, I had

the time freedom to work with other moms who had the time freedom, except for caregiving. We were often in a leadership position of a lot of movements for social justice because we had our basic need covered as single parents. My housing subsidy and income benefits through the Ontario Disability Support Program kept me afloat during gaps in grants for many years.

Grey says a basic income would provide more people with the resources and time freedom to pursue advocacy, capacity building, and sustainable development in their communities. She says that with climate change already causing harm in vulnerable communities, this work is more crucial than ever:

> A basic income would make all the difference to everybody. How could anybody possibly fully engage in transforming their community, or their work, or their organization if they are working all the time? It's gotten harder and harder for people to engage as the work-life balance has worsened. What I find now is that I'm lucky to have a couple of people maintain a vision. Everyone else churns in and out as their lives throw them off the track of advocacy. It's hard, and painful, and hurtful to be trying to build new solutions and ideas when the people who created those with you, and are dedicated and want to do it as well, can't continue to work with you because they have to feed their kids, they have to get a house, have to move cities, have to find more paid work.

Grey says she's living proof of how a basic income could help:

> I had the great fortune to get rent-geared-to-income. As soon as I got rent-geared-to-income status, which has been my version of something akin to a basic income, it meant that whether I was making a lot or a little, my housing was

safe. When you have five kids, that's everything. Because I had rent-geared-to-income, I didn't have to spend all my time working and then stacking this unpaid work onto my paid work life.

She also considers a basic income as an anti-racist policy:

> In any marginalized community a basic income makes all the difference in the world because it's distinctly different insofar as you're not having to live a certain way and present yourself in a certain way in order to maintain eligibility for social services. It gives you a lot more freedom to make choices. Because of this, it's the ultimate anti-racist policy. It's not the only thing we need to do, but it would make a giant difference.

Grey says Martin Luther King Jr's advocacy has inspired much of her work in promoting basic income as a human right, and she says a basic income is a key part of ensuring that everyone is able to live a life with dignity.

Martin Luther King Jr advocated for a basic income in the years following the civil rights movement. Much of King's work and his plea for a basic income were rooted in human rights. In 1967, the last year of his life, King started what was known as the "Poor People's Campaign" to address some of the shortcomings of the civil rights movement.[7] The campaign was launched in an effort to raise the standard of living for Americans, especially African Americans, living in poverty, and to advocate for economic equality. King understood that Black and Indigenous peoples and people of colour were largely being excluded from the labour market, and in order to reach substantive equality, there needed to be economic justice. The Poor People's Campaign requested that the US federal government pass a $30 billion anti-poverty bill, which would have included a guaranteed basic income for all Americans.[8]

Grey says:

> The first and foremost principle of human rights is the right to self-determination. You can't have that if you can't cover your basic needs. If your basic needs are reliant on if Walmart is going to employ you as a greeter, then you do not have your human rights. Even if you work at a very well-paying job, and you're making oodles of money but you have no time at all with your family, no time to garden, no time to be healthy, you don't have your human rights then either.

Basic income will not eliminate systemic racism in the labour market, but it can ensure that people's basic needs are met, uphold their human rights, and provide people with the time and resources to work towards real solutions in areas of life that need improvement.

"To me, [income insecurity] is the worst violation of human rights," says Grey. "All of it comes down to precarity—being unable to invest one's time wisely—and the chronic lack of security. All of it comes down to a lack of your basic needs being met. To me, getting a basic income worldwide is a race against time for the survival of our species."

Gender and Precarious Work

Gender is also associated with precarious work. Women are underpaid relative to men. A study by the Canadian Women's Foundation shows that for every hour worked, women earn on average 13 per cent less than men. But women also tend to work fewer hours than men. Comparing total earnings, women earn 67 cents for every dollar men earn, and the gaps are larger for racialized and Indigenous women. [9] As a consequence, women are more at risk of falling into poverty.

The relationship between gender and low wages is a complex one that touches on ideas about the roles of men and women in society that have developed over centuries and become so entrenched that they are often not recognized. For example, care work is seen as a female domain, and most of the care work provided in society is not provided through the market but rather through the unpaid labour of daughters, wives, sisters, and mothers. Even though 83.5 per cent of working-age women either worked for pay or were seeking paid work in 2019, the expectation that they would continue to provide a disproportionate share of unpaid work persisted.[11]

Women working full time for pay rarely have jobs that allow them to provide the many hours of unpaid work their mothers and grandmothers provided. Therefore, daycare centres and nursing homes have expanded to provide child and elder care that previous generations might have provided in the home. Much of the labour that allows these organizations to operate comes from women. The women providing care work for pay are often precariously employed and paid low wages because this kind of work continues to be seen as women's work that has traditionally been invisible and unpaid.

When COVID-19 shut down schools and imposed restrictions on daycares, the social expectation that women would somehow deal with the children was not consistent with the notion that women should also work full time for pay. The central role of daycare workers could not be ignored any longer.

In Canada, according to the Child Care Human Resources Sector Council, more than 96 per cent of child-care workers and early childhood educators are women, and they are low-income earners whether they work in non-profit or for-profit centres.[12]

Dr. Susan Prentice, professor of sociology at the University of Manitoba, said child-care workers and early childhood educators in Canada earn something under $20 an hour. "We very clearly exploit the women who take care of our children," says Prentice.

The Personal Cost of Care Work

Maddy Turbett has a passion for helping people. She decided to pursue a career in care because it allowed her to make connections with others. "My whole life, ever since I was a little kid, I've wanted to help people. That's what I said I wanted to do when I grew up and that stayed the same ... so that was a path that seemed inevitable."

A little over three years ago, Turbett started working as a child-care assistant at a non-profit child-care centre in Winnipeg. She was responsible for planning and coordinating activities, making meals, and tending to the children at the after-school program. "I made so many amazing connections and I really enjoyed my time with the people around me. As stressful as it could get, the hugs you would get from kids when they were looking for comfort and you knew they were finding comfort in the relationship you had, it made it all worth it," she says.

Turbett says child care plays a crucial part in society, but she felt undervalued in her role. "I think I was underpaid," says Turbett. Her starting pay was $11.50 per hour and increased only to $11.96 in the two years she worked in a child-care facility. At the time, she was earning only 31 cents above minimum wage in Manitoba. She was making an annual salary of about $18,000; this is well below the poverty line, which is $21,000 after tax for a single person without children.[13]

Turbett says because of her low annual salary at the child-care centre, she had to take on additional respite work in order to make ends meet. "I felt like I was going above and beyond and I knew there was no money for me. I've always been told by people in my life, 'you don't go into childcare for the money.' If you can't get the money, why are you there? You still have to support yourself," she says. "I was lucky that I was living with a partner, but I did respite on the side to supplement my income. I was living with my [husband] and we shared expenses in a one-bedroom apartment, but it wasn't sustainable for the rest of my life."

Turbett left her position at the child-care facility to pursue other work because her salary wouldn't have allowed her to pursue her dreams of buying a house and starting a family.

"Leaving the kids broke my heart. You build such a close relationship with them. I had kids crying because I was leaving and parents who just didn't believe it because I was a huge part of their kids' lives for almost three years.... They treated me like a valued member of their lives, like I was family, but you don't let family just live on $18,000 a year," she says.

Turbett says she's frustrated that it took a pandemic for care workers to be recognized for their work. She said care workers have always been essential. "If we were so essential, we should get funding, we should be better paid. Now that the lens is focused on us, people should realize that the care economy is who helps your children when they're young. They essentially help raise your children. They're the people who take care of the most vulnerable people in society," she says.

A basic income alone won't solve the gender wage gap, but it can recognize the value of reproductive and home-based care work, while also giving women who work for pay in the care sector an income they can live on. Basic income, of course, is not the final answer to gender inequality in the labour market. But as in the case of other inequities, basic income allows women, and others, to work towards gender equality.

For Turbett, a basic income could have allowed her to continue working with kids, a job she loved. "I would love to be able to come home and have my evenings free because I'm not worried about saving and getting by. I wasn't able to save any money when I was at the daycare, but knowing that I could still be a part of that community and also know that my needs are being met, that's huge," she says.

Newcomers and the Precariat

In June and July 2019, fire inspectors found 88 workers living in five houses in Kingston, Ontario. An inspector was told by someone at the property that there were more residents but the first shift had already left. A range of fire and building violations was documented, including unsafe cooking facilities. These workers had come from China to work at the Royal Milk Plant on visas reserved for workers with expertise "of significant economic benefit to Canada."[14]

Newcomers to Canada are also overrepresented among those with low-paid precarious work. The terms "migrant workers," "asylum seekers," "refugees," "foreign workers," and "immigrants" are all used interchangeably in ordinary conversation, but there are important differences in the opportunities and barriers different categories of workers face.

In 2019, 341,180 permanent residents were admitted to Canada, 58 per cent of whom were invited on the basis of a lengthy process that prioritized immigrants with education and language skills that would allow them to work and support themselves and their families in Canada.[15] Another 91,311 were admitted as family members of established immigrants. In the same year, 48,530 refugees and protected persons were admitted. "Refugees" or "asylum seekers" are people who cannot or will not return to their home country because of a justifiable fear of persecution. If they are sponsored by governments, they have access to income support through the Resettlement Assistance Program for up to a year at rates similar to provincial income assistance. If they are privately sponsored, the sponsors are responsible for income support. While provincial arrangements vary across the country, most provinces will allow a successful refugee claimant to apply for provincial income assistance if they have no other means of support, but this support is not available before their case is decided.

People who arrive as permanent residents, particularly refugees or asylum seekers, sometimes take time to settle into the local labour market. According to the 2016 census, immigrants who had arrived within the previous five years had a low-income rate of 31.4 per cent and had an average total income that was 63 per cent of that of a non-immigrant.[16] For most, this is a temporary situation and, as they acclimatize to the Canadian labour market and gain local experience, their earning potential will increase.

One particular hardship faced by many immigrants is that, although they were invited to Canada because of their educational attainments, they soon find that their credentials are not necessarily recognized by local employers. Some professionals face significant financial and bureaucratic challenges in having their licences recognized. Many foreign-trained physicians, for example, are required to participate in a residency before they are permitted to practise, but few provinces make access simple. Educational programs required for qualification may carry hefty fees. Throughout all of this, an applicant faces an urgent need to provide for their family. As a consequence, we have a very well-educated Uber and taxi-driving workforce because these jobs are accessible. Many immigrants are forced by financial necessity to take on precarious work rather than committing time and resources to having their credentials recognized. A basic income would ease their financial burden and allow applicants the time and resources to make decisions with a better long-term payoff.

By contrast, many people arrive in Canada to work with temporary visas, like the Royal Milk Plant workers. Some of these are relatively high-paid workers who enter under international mobility provisions, but some arrive as part of the Temporary Foreign Worker Program (TFWP). In 2019, 98,310 workers were admitted under the provisions of the TFWP.[17] Unlike immigrants and refugee claimants, they are admitted to Canada for fixed periods of time to work for specific employers. Traditionally, a large proportion arrived as live-in caregivers. During the pandemic, the plight of agricultural workers, 20 per cent of whom arrived under the TFWP, has been highlighted but their experiences are far from unique.

These workers labour under particular constraints. They often arrive in Canada on visas tied to a particular employer, making it difficult for them to change jobs or quit, if their rights are violated, without risking deportation. In the case of live-in caregivers, this is exacerbated by the fact that many live in their employers' homes. There is no easy route to citizenship. Applicants need two years of work experience to apply for permanent resident status, and the nature of their contracts makes this particularly difficult to attain. In the meantime, they are not eligible for provincial or federal income assistance of any kind if their work relationship breaks down or they become ill and unable to work. Workers under the TFWP are admitted to Canada on the attestation of employers that there is a labour shortage and therefore they are expected to be working. While their work is covered by labour legislation, enforcing their rights is challenging. Their status in the country is dependent on the goodwill of their employers, who can threaten them with deportation.

These workers have been treated as disposable by the Canadian economy. Their invitation to Canada is based on evidence of a labour shortage provided by potential employers. The idea of a labour shortage, however, is not without controversy. A labour shortage means that employers cannot hire as much labour as they would like to hire at the wage they would like to pay. There are many people who are already residents in Canada without jobs; if employers cannot hire them, it is usually because workers with other options won't work in the conditions provided for the wage offered. If employers paid more or offered better conditions of employment, the shortage would disappear. It's hard not to see the TFWP as exploitation, even if workers willingly accept the job offer.

Employers often point to the contribution their businesses make to the Canadian economy, arguing that if they paid workers more or improved the terms of employment, they would have to raise prices and no one would buy their products. Or they would have to automate, and there would be no jobs at all. This, they argue, would hurt the very workers who are fleeing even worse conditions in their home countries to take these opportunities in Canada.

When the pandemic spread across the country, one of the largest outbreaks occurred at Cargill meat-packing plants in Alberta,[18] later followed by similar outbreaks at meat-packing and processing plants across the country. Most of the employees were in Canada as part of the TFWP. Cargill argued that it was not responsible for the outbreak; it pointed out that many of its employees lived in overcrowded housing many kilometres away in Calgary and travelled in overcrowded vehicles to get to work. This, they argued, and not the conditions on the plant floor, was responsible for the infection rate. However, few people choose to live in substandard housing or travel several kilometres to work in uncomfortable vehicles when they can afford better. The employer must take some responsibility for the quality of life that its compensation allows.

This country has a responsibility to not use its TFWP to exploit workers who are vulnerable because of the conditions in their home countries. Employers use the TFWP to keep a lid on Canadian wage rates. If they had to rely on Canadian labour, they would raise their wages. If their threat of automation is valid, perhaps the jobs being eliminated are jobs that no one should have to do. If their fear that no one will pay more for their products is valid, then consumers will have demonstrated that we do not value the product enough to pay what it costs to produce it. We will have signalled through the market that we prefer to do without. The TFWP is, by its very nature, exploitative.

If we care about opportunities for the people we hire through this program, we would do well to admit them to the country through our standard immigration quotas.

If the TFWP remains, and all political parties have capitulated to the demands of would-be employers, then at minimum we need to enforce labour legislation and be certain that workers have access to supports to ensure that their rights are recognized. There should be a clear path to permanent residency for those who want it, and visas should not be tied to a single employer. Most important of all, those who employ workers under the TFWP should be forced to pay into an insurance plan to meet the needs of workers who become disabled or who cannot return home but cannot work, as was the case for many during the COVID-19 outbreak. These workers, like all other residents of Canada, should be able to live a life with dignity.

Bottom Line

A basic income doesn't let employers and governments off the hook when it comes to improving working conditions and wages in the paid labour market. However, it does create the possibility of social change. When people aren't worrying about where their next meal is coming from, or how they're going to pay for housing each month, they have the chance to think about tackling bigger problems.

A basic income would also improve working conditions by allowing people to go back to school or to take additional training programs without having to worry about surviving paycheque to paycheque. This is especially important for newcomers, who many require time and resources to have their credentials recognized. One important outcome of the short-lived Basic Income Guarantee pilot project in Ontario was that the quality of jobs held by low-wage workers seemed to improve. Instead of short-term, precarious, and poorly paid work, basic income allowed workers to search for jobs with better benefits and prospects.[19]

References

[1] John Clarke, "Basic Income Is Not the Answer to the Crisis," *Spring Magazine: A Magazine of Socialist Ideas in Action* (March 21, 2020), https://springmag.ca/basic-income-is-not-the-answer-to-the-crisis

[2] Evelyn L. Forget, *Basic income for Canadians: From the COVID-19 Emergency to Financial Security for All* (Toronto: Lormier, 2020), 141.

[3] Ibid.

[4] St. James Town Service Providers' Network, *2016 Neighbourhood Profile: North St. James Town*, 2016, 1–22, https://www.toronto.ca/ext/sdfa/Neighbourhood%20Profiles/pdf/2016/pdf1/cpa74.pdf

[5] Ibid.

[6] Ibid.

[7] Nina Aron, "As One of His Final Acts, Martin Luther King Fought for a Basic Income for All," *Timeline* (April 2, 2018), https://timeline.com/mlk-wanted-universal-basic-income-as-his-last-campaign-b0ba61aa77b8

[8] Ibid.

[9] Canadian Women's Foundation, *The Facts about the Gender Pay Gap in Canada*, n.d., https://canadianwomen.org/the-facts/the-gender-pay-gap/

[11] Statistics Canada, *Gender, Diversity and Inclusion Statistics*, 2020, https://www.statcan.gc.ca/eng/topics-start/gender_diversity_and_inclusion

[12] Child Care Human Resources Sector Council, *A Portrait of Canada's Early Childhood Education and Care (ECEC) Workforce*, 2009, 3–5, http://www.ccsc-cssge.ca/sites/default/files/uploads/Projects-Pubs-Docs/1.1portraitbrochure_e.pdf

[13] Campaign 2000, *2019 Report Card on Child and Family Poverty in Canada*, 2019, 6, https://campaign2000.ca/wp-content/uploads/2020/01/campaign-2000-report-setting-the-stage-for-a-poverty-free-canada-january-14-2020.pdf

[14] Janyce McGregor, "Foreign Workers Assigned Unsafe Housing During Contracts at Ontario Baby Formula Plant: Documents", *CBC News*, April 12, 2021. https://www.cbc.ca/news/politics/foreign-workers-milk-plant-1.5967593

[15] Immigration, Refugees and Citizenship Canada, *Annual Report to Parliament, 2019*, https://www.canada.ca/en/immigration-refugees-citizenship/corporate/publications-manuals/annual-report-parliament-immigration-2020.html

[16] Forget, *Basic Income*, 145.

[17] Immigration, Refugees and Citizenship Canada, *Annual Report to Parliament, 2019*, https://www.canada.ca/en/immigration-refugees-citizenship/corporate/publications-manuals/annual-report-parliament-immigration-2020.html

[18] Jason Herring, "COVID-19 Outbreak Declared at New Cargill Plant as Alberta Reports 84 New Cases Province-Wide," *Calgary Herald*, August 14, 2020, https://calgaryherald.com/news/local-news/outbreak-declared-at-new-cargill-plant-as-84-new-cases-reported

[19] Hugh Segal, Evelyn Forget, and Keith Banting, *A Federal Basic Income within the Post COVID-19 Economic Recovery Plan* (Ottawa: Royal Society of Canada, 2020), 9, https://rsc-src.ca/en/research-and-reports/covid-19-policy-briefing/federal-basic-income-within-post-covid-19-economic

6

Living with Disabilities

Disability policy in Canada has been described as "conflicting," "fragmented," "confusing," and "inaccessible."[1] Most income support available to people with disabilities is a patchwork of legislation, rules, providers, and benefits that requires considerable patience to understand and navigate.[2]

Many people with disabilities rely on income support administered by provinces and territories. Programs vary considerably across Canada, based on how disabilities are medically certified; how much money people receive; how (and whether) benefits are indexed; and the regulations on allowable assets and monthly earnings, and how benefits are clawed back when people earn other income.[3]

For example, in Manitoba, disability benefits are offered through Employment and Income Assistance (EIA), which also provides support for working-age people without disabilities. A study by the Department of Families showed that in 2018, a single adult without children could receive up to $1,012 per month.[4] In Alberta, benefits levels are more generous. Support for some people with disabilities is administered through the Assured Income for the Severely Handicapped (AISH) program. A report from this program showed that a living allowance for a single adult without children is a maximum of $1,685 per month.[5] However, cuts have been proposed for this program.

Most provincial income benefits for people with disabilities include coverage for additional costs like medication; assistive devices like voice recognition programs, hearing aids, and wheelchairs; and vision care. In many cases, these health-related supports are covered, or partially covered, by provincial income programs. These additional supports are important. However, a problem emerges for low-income earners who may have similar needs. In most provinces, working people do not qualify for these supports if they are not accessing provincial income benefits. This creates a barrier for those who can work. By accepting a job, people with disabilities risk losing access to important health care.

There are also federal benefits available to people with disabilities, which include the Disability Tax Credit and the Registered Disability Savings Plan. Some people who have worked in the past receive disability support through the Canada or Quebec pension plans. Each of these programs has different qualification processes. The slough of income support programs available both provincially and federally is complex to navigate and all programs require individual applications, which are lengthy and oftentimes intrusive. A national population-based survey showed that the majority of disabled social assistance recipients rarely access additional benefits for which they might be eligible.[6] This contributes to a cycle of poverty.

People with disabilities are far more likely to live in poverty than Canadians without disabilities. According to Statistics Canada, the highest rates of poverty for people aged 15 to 64 years old are among those with severe disabilities who live alone.[7] People with disabilities also comprise the majority of social assistance recipients in Canada.[8] One in five Canadians report having one or more disabilities that limit their daily activities.[9]

Most provincial assistance benefits provide an income well below the poverty line in Canada. However, working full time is not always an option for people with disabilities. Those on social assistance who take on some type of work often find that their disability income support is dramatically reduced or disappears altogether as soon as they earn a few extra hundred dollars a month. However, it is often the loss of additional benefits, such as prescription drugs in many provinces, that is more devastating. If a new job pays enough to make someone ineligible for provincial income support, these additional benefits also disappear. Many people with disabilities have significant medical-related expenses that no one earning close to minimum wage could afford to pay, and even those without such needs might hesitate to take a job that puts such additional benefits at risk in case their condition worsens or severe needs recur.

Provincial disability programs usually require two assessments: a medical diagnosis to be completed by a doctor, and a second assessment that demonstrates that the disability is significant and interferes with the applicant's ability to work or go to school, or substantially interferes with daily living. Often the outcome of these assessments depends on the skill of the clinician at completing forms, as assessing disability can be subjective. People sometimes apply for the programs several times before they are successful, particularly people with episodic or invisible disabilities. The bureaucracies are better at understanding physical disabilities that require accommodation than they are at assessing mental health issues that can be just as debilitating. There are entire agencies that exist to help people document the ways in which their disability interferes with their daily lives, and to help medical practitioners complete the forms in ways that bureaucrats will understand. This is a draining, time-consuming process for everyone.

Current income support programs for people with disabilities are a no-win, says disability advocate and author Al Etmanski:

> It's inadequate practically, and functionally, it's designed from a welfare perspective which assumes you're going to cheat the system. The regulatory framework, the application process, the mistrust, and the monitoring. It's very

expensive for the system and taxpayer, and very insulting for the individual. Essentially, people with disabilities have a double whammy with the system: there's the systemic discrimination because you have a disability, and there is the systemic discrimination our society has built into our welfare apparatus.

"You're Trapped in Poverty"

Amanda Robar survives on just $895 per month. She has been a recipient of the Ontario Disability Support Program (ODSP) for the past seventeen years. "It's hard juggling the finances," she says. "You're cutting corners the best you can, always looking for savings. Sometimes it's shopping for no-name products rather than President's Choice. You're shopping for anything that's cheaper."

Robar lives with multiple medical conditions including rheumatoid arthritis, alopecia, anxiety, and depression. Robar's most serious condition is epilepsy:

> I have had epilepsy my entire life. My epilepsy is unpredictable. I could be fine for hours and then have a bunch of seizures. Most of my seizures cause me to go temporarily blind. They can progress into bigger ones where my left hand begins to shake. Some nights I will have seizures during my sleep. My seizures take a toll on my entire body. I get tired and need to take a nap for two hours or more. Some days are better than others after recovery.

Robar's epilepsy and other conditions prevent her from holding down long-term paid employment. "There are people who physically or mentally cannot work," she says, "Those medical conditions are beyond their control. Some things there is no cure for. There is no cure for epilepsy. Some conditions deteriorate as well. Until you walk in their shoes you don't know what their life is like."

As a result of Robar's complex conditions, she relies on ODSP to cover her basic needs. However, she says the system is complicated and frustrating to navigate: "[ODSP] digs really deep into your personal life.... I felt frustrated, embarrassed, angry, and sorry for my doctor who had to fill out a pile of papers each time I reapplied. It is a hassle for all involved; the person applying, their family, the caseworker, and the applicant's family doctor ... my epilepsy isn't going away," she says.

Robar says it's difficult trying to find out what coverage and benefits she's entitled to:

> When the people who work in the [ODSP] office can't even find the information themselves, that's just sad. I've spent hours on the computer trying to find information on the website. The system is just overwhelming. I think I've met one person who can locate a piece of information the whole time I've been on ODSP. I've lost track of how many caseworkers I have had. Trying to get in touch with my caseworker is beyond frustrating. I will phone and leave a message and wait a week. Then I will phone again and leave a second message. I've had a few caseworkers who will get back to me, but the majority I've had don't bother.

She requires coverage for additional health aids, the most important of these being a service dog. She explains:

> Kramer was my first service dog. He gave me the confidence to travel places independently. When I got Kramer, I was having complex partial seizures where I would wander about with no destination and my brain just went on autopilot. Kramer made sure I didn't wander out into the street, and would find a seat for me to sit on to recover. Kira [my current service dog] was taught these skills as well, as they are very important. She is also trained to push an emergency button should I go into a tonic-clonic seizure and not be

able to get my emergency medication myself. This button will call my mother first. Kira was also taught to take me home if I was disoriented after a seizure. Due to my seizures and lack of peripheral vision, I cannot drive, so I take public transportation. Kira seems to know when the bus is arriving before I can see it. She knows the way around both by bus and on foot…. My life changed dramatically once Kramer and Kira came into it. I became more independent and felt safer staying out later. This may not seem like much to some people, but to me this was huge. The simple act of stroking my service dogs helps with my anxiety both during a seizure and while around crowds. Both Kramer and Kira have helped me cope with my depression. I still have rough days where I feel overwhelmed, but knowing my companion is by my side helps me get through the day.

Having a service dog is an essential part of Robar's day-to-day life. However, she says ODSP gives her only an additional $84 per month to help cover the added expense of caring for a service dog. Any other costs come out of her budget for basic needs. On average, Robar says, she spends about $231 per month on Kira's food, grooming, and insurance fees. On top of that, Kira goes in for a yearly check-up at a cost of more than $200. Soon, Robar will be getting a new service dog as Kira is near retirement, a cost also not covered by ODSP.

"All service dogs come to a point in their life when it is time for them to retire. Kira is nearing this stage, which means it is time for a new puppy to start training. The cost of two years of training a service dog is around $36,000. This covers boarding, training, food, and grooming. Not to mention additional costs such as insurance, vet bills and any unexpected emergencies," she says.

Robar and her family had to set up a GoFundMe page to seek community financial help in order to pay for Robar's new service dog, Cable.

Clawbacks Keep People in a Cycle of Poverty

Despite the low assistance levels Robar manages to survive on, she says the most demeaning aspect of ODSP is that earned income is clawed back. In Ontario, the maximum someone can earn is $200 over the monthly ODSP payment; if you make more than that, the program claws back 50 per cent of additional earnings.[11]

"ODSP will give you a $100 work allowance, which is great if you can work," says Robar. She has worked part time while living on ODSP in the past, but between her complex medical needs and clawback rates, working makes her worse off both financially and health-wise, she explains:

> If someone asked me if I wanted to work, I would say yes. It's the clawback that makes it impossible. You are trapped in poverty; you can't get ahead. ODSP forces you to stay stuck in one position. It's not something that I choose. I require my medication to be covered, but should I earn too much, I risk the chance of losing my benefits. There are things we [people with disabilities] need covered, and with the money being taken away, it's not helpful.

Etmanski says clawbacks are designed to keep people poor. Under ODSP, the asset ceiling for a single person without children is only $40,000.[12]

"There is no incentive to get ahead, no incentive to save in the way other Canadians have the opportunity to save for their future, make investments, create a plan for education or home ownership," he says. "I would say that the current system is both broken and is based on false assumptions. It's based on inaccurate assumptions about people with disabilities. That has to be understood because no matter how much reform takes place, it's still chained to those original assumptions."

Like everyone, people with disabilities have aspirations and make plans for their future. Yet the current system assumes that someone with a disability will always require someone else to take care of them and to make their decisions for them. The system is set up to do that. Anyone who doesn't fit that stereotype is assumed to not be genuinely disabled and therefore not in need of financial or other assistance. The disability system itself enforces a kind of dependence and actively interferes with autonomy and self-respect.

Disability Benefits and the Canada Pension Plan

Provincial disability benefits are designed to be programs of last resort. That means that everyone is required to exhaust every other source of income before they apply to the province. A recent Manitoba court case demonstrated how this design harms recipients.

Martin Stadler, a recipient of EIA disability benefits in Manitoba, was cut off from provincial income support when he turned 60 years old. Because he had previously worked, Stadler was entitled to a pension from the Canada Pension Plan (CPP). The normal date for receiving CPP is at age 65, but someone can apply as early as age 60 to receive a pension, although the monthly amount will be 36 per cent lower for the rest of their life. If they wait until age 70 to begin their pension, the monthly amount received is higher for the rest of their life. Sadler was issued a letter from the province informing him that under the Manitoba Assistance Act, he was required to start receiving CPP payments at age 60.

From the perspective of the province, Stadler could receive a pension at age 60 and therefore he was expected to apply for it, even though he would be financially penalized by CPP for doing so. People who are not receiving disability benefits have the right to decide for themselves when they want to begin receiving their pension.

The question before the court was: Does requiring a disabled recipient of income assistance to apply for CPP retirement benefits early, at age 60 instead of age 65, infringe on their equality rights under the Charter of Rights and Freedoms?

Stadler argued that because he is disabled, he was not given the same choice or option as an employable, able-bodied person regarding CPP. He argued that as a result of regulations within the Manitoba Assistance Act, he was discriminated against because he was disabled and a recipient of income assistance. The regulation in question under the Manitoba Assistance Act states that a recipient of income assistance must make all reasonable efforts to obtain the maximum amount of compensation, benefits, or contributions to support themselves under another Act or program, which includes federal income support schemes.[13]

Because EIA is a program of last resort, the Social Service Appeal Board, a mechanism in place to hear individual complaints against EIA and other social services, upheld its decision to discontinue Stadler's assistance payments based on the provision in the Act. The Appeal Board argued that the requirement to access other available financial resources is part of an overall system of benefits meant to address the needs of people with disabilities, but it does not create a disadvantage, or perpetuate discrimination or prejudice.

The judge sided with Stadler, and he won the case in the Manitoba Court of Appeal. The verdict stated that forcing disabled social assistance recipients to apply early for CPP benefits is discriminatory and may condemn them to poverty for the rest of their lives. The final decision was appealed by the province all the way up to the Supreme Court, but the Supreme Court refused to hear the appeal, meaning Stadler won the case there, too.[14]

Basic Income for People with Disabilities

Etmanski says reforming current systems is not enough to ensure equity for people with disabilities in Canada:

> The only solution, in my opinion, is the transformation in how we provide income support to Canadians who are

poor. To me, that's basic income. Everything else we try to do—minimizing the clawbacks, maximizing the asset limit, and all of the other policing that takes place—they're all designed to destroy people's soul. So, tinkering with the design of these sends the message that you're unworthy. It's time to shift to a transformational strategy as opposed to incremental reform.

Robar agrees. She says a basic income would provide her with more opportunities: "Basic income would provide every Canadian with the money to live a dignified life and that's something every human being has the right to. Why not just make basic income a reality? With basic income it wouldn't be so much of a struggle for me. You get stuck in limbo where I'm at."

Robar, who's now 36 years old, won't qualify for any additional income support until she turns 65, at which point she will be eligible for Old Age Security (OAS) and the Guaranteed Income Supplement (GIS). To put that in perspective, Robar will be living below the poverty line on ODSP for another twenty-six years—and she will still be under the poverty line with OAS and GIS, unless those programs are made more generous.

"I'm in an age category where there is nothing extra for me," she says.

> I'm not a senior so I don't get senior discounts, a pension, or the Guaranteed Income Supplement, and I don't have kids so I don't get the Canada Child Benefit. I only get ODSP and the Disability Tax Credit. The government needs to boost income levels for people like me. If I wanted to take any class or recreational activity, it would cost me the full amount. I've asked around to see if anyone offers a lower cost for people on disability support and they don't. It really sucks. Other people who have kids can put their kids through classes, and seniors can take a painting class

for a cheaper cost, but for someone like me, I can't afford to do anything like that. I'm already crunching my budget. Why can't it be more equal?

Authors Daniel Beland and Pierre-Marc Daigneault argue that people with disabilities are living on the bare minimum of income, and many don't qualify, or are not accessing, additional federal benefits: "The stark reality is that the majority of Canadians with a disability who receive social assistance receive no other public income benefit at the same time. There is relatively little stacking or simultaneous adding together of benefits that would help offset 'the low individual payment levels' of provincial social assistance for people with disabilities."[15]

Basic income is the only way forward in providing support for people with disabilities in order to ensure equality and restore dignity, says Etmanski:

> Basic income would allow [people with disabilities] to get up in the morning and go about their day knowing that they have a base of income support to rely on. Most of us almost can't imagine that. We think about the challenges at work, about the contributions we're going to make, but people with disabilities have to start from another point of view. How are they going to make do? How are they going to survive? ...There are already enough challenges for a person with disabilities around accessibility and other barriers in income support, so to be able to eliminate part of that [with basic income] ... it will liberate people's soul. It's not just the functional benefit of money, it's also the implications of the current system and what it does to people, it beats people down and it chains them.

There is often a false assumption that basic income is a replacement for other benefits or publicly funded services. For people with disabilities, basic income is not a substitute for access to pharmaceuticals, assistive devices, or any other services that are essential. However, it would be more equitable and efficient to provide these supports through the health-care system or to make them dependent on the level of someone's income rather than its source. This way, low-income workers would also have access to these benefits, and people with disabilities who want to work would not be prevented from doing so.

Robar says a basic income would allow her to pursue her passions and live a fuller life: "I would love to write a book or do an anthology with a few people, but the cost is expensive. Right now, I can't afford that. Saving for travel would be great, too. Every year my family would go down to Disneyland for an epilepsy awareness event and my parents would have to cover me. I would like to do that independently. So, knowing that [basic income] is there, and is being saved, would be great."

COVID-19 and People with Disabilities

The COVID-19 pandemic impacted people from all socio-economic backgrounds, but the government response was particularly infuriating for people with disabilities. Many faced higher costs because some of the organizations they had relied on to supplement their disability cheques struggled to provide services during the lockdown. Yet financial support for people with disabilities was not a priority for any level of government.

People with disabilities accessing provincial income support were ineligible for the Canadian Emergency Response Benefit (CERB) and were also excluded from the Canada Recovery Benefit (CRB).

Robar says:

> I was angry in a way because in my mind this is what basic income would help with. You're saying to everybody else,

> "Here you go, here's $2,000," but you're saying to people with disabilities, "Suck it up and live on less than $1,000." How fair is that when you could easily say, "Let's look at all of Canada and give a basic income to those who need it." CERB could have easily been transitioned to a basic income, but that hasn't happened.

It wasn't until several months into the pandemic, and the CERB, that the government announced financial support for "extraordinary expenses faced by persons with disabilities during the COVID-19 pandemic."[16] The government promised a non-taxable, non-reportable, one-time payment of up to $600. However, only those who qualified for and received the Disability Tax Credit were eligible. This parameter excluded many people with disabilities who received provincial support but had not applied for the federal Disability Tax Credit.

"I was frustrated at how [the government] talked about jobs, the work sector, and getting the economy up and running, but it wasn't until near the end of the summer that they said, 'Hey, wait a minute, what about these people with disabilities?'" says Robar.

In the 2020 Speech from the Throne, Prime Minister Justin Trudeau announced a new benefit for people with disabilities called the Canada Disability Benefit. The benefit would, he said, be modelled after the GIS, but no details were provided about how this benefit would work and who would be deemed eligible.[17] Nevertheless, Etmanski is optimistic about the prospect of added support, but says there is work to be done to ensure that people with disabilities are consulted and included in the process:

> The announcement in the Throne Speech is the result of a lot of people over a lot of time saying we're got to do something really fundamental. It's a turning point opportunity be to grabbed, to be celebrated, to be worked on, to be strategic

about. To the best of my knowledge, no government in the world has made a declaration that commits to doing something about poverty for people with disabilities, that's historic in Canada and anywhere in the world. It's overdue.

It remains to be seen whether this declaration from the government will be followed up with action.

References

[1] Mary Ann McColl, Atul Jaiswal, Shannon Jones, Lynn Roberts, and Caitlin Murphy, *A Review of Disability Policy in Canada*, Canadian Disability Policy Alliance, 2017, 7, http://www.disabilitypolicyalliance.ca/wp-content/uploads/2018/01/A-Review-of-Disability-Policy-in-Canada-3rd-edition-Final-1-1.pdf

[2] Ibid., 7.

[3] Daniel Beland and Pierre-Marc Daigneault, *Welfare Reform in Canada: Provincial Social Assistance in Comparative Perspectives* (Toronto: University of Toronto Press, 2015), 294, https://books-scholarsportal-info.uml.idm.oclc.org/en/read?id=/ebooks/ebooks3/utpress/2015-12-22/1/9781442609730#page=1

[4] Department of Families, Government of Manitoba, "Employment and Income Assistance for Persons with Disabilities," 2018, https://www.gov.mb.ca/fs/eia/eia_disability.html

[5] Government of Alberta, Assured Income for the Severely Handicapped (AISH), *AISH Program Policy*, http://www.humanservices.alberta.ca/AWOnline/AISH/7242.html

[6] Beland and Daigneault, *Welfare Reform*, 297.

[7] Statistics Canada, *The Daily—Canadian Survey on Disabilities, 2017*, https://www150.statcan.gc.ca/n1/daily-quotidien/181128/dq181128a-eng.htm

[8] Beland and Daigneault, *Welfare Reform*, 294.

[9] Statistics Canada, *The Daily, 2017.*

[10] Evelyn L. Forget, *Basic Income for Canadians: The Key to a Healthier, Happier, and More Secure Life for All* (Toronto: Lorimer, 2018), 122.

[11] Government of Ontario, Ministry of Children, Community and Social Services, "ODSP: Information Sheet," n.d., https://www.mcss.gov.on.ca/en/mcss/programs/social/odsp/info_sheets/employment_supports.aspx

[12] Government of Ontario, Ministry of Children, Community and Social Services, *Ontario Disability Support Program—Income Support,* n.d., https://www.mcss.gov.on.ca/en/mcss/programs/social/directives/odsp/is/4_1_ODSP_ISDirectives.aspx#:~:text=particular%20benefit%20unit.-,Asset%20Limits,for%20a%20particular%20benefit%20unit

[13] *Stadler v Director, St Boniface/St Vital* (2020), MBCA 46, p. 2, http://www.socialrights.ca/2020/Stadler.pdf

[14] The Supreme Court will hear this case through 2020 and 2021.

[15] Beland and Daigneault, *Welfare Reform,* 297.

[16] Government of Canada, "One-Time Payment to Persons with Disabilities," 2020, https://www.canada.ca/en/services/benefits/covid19-emergency-benefits/one-time-payment-persons-disabilities.html

[17] Government of Canada, "A Stronger and More Resilient Canada," Speech from the Throne, September 2020, https://www.canada.ca/en/privy-council/campaigns/speech-throne/2020/stronger-resilient-canada.html

7

Violence Against Women and Gender-Diverse People

Violence against women is a major public health issue and one of the greatest human rights violations. Between 2019 and 2020, nearly 243 million women and girls worldwide have been victims of sexual, emotional, or physical violence by an intimate partner.[1]

Violence and income insecurity are intrinsically linked. Canadians living in low-income households are more likely to be victims of violent crimes than those in higher income households.[2] Women make up the majority of Canada's income-insecure population, according to the Public Health Agency of Canada.

Poverty and violence are a toxic mix in women's lives. Poverty marginalizes women, which in turn increases their risk of victimization. Violence also isolates women, as the mental and physical impacts negatively affect their sense of well-being.[3]

In Canada, violence disproportionally impacts First Nations, Inuit, and Métis women, girls, and Two Spirit persons. In 2014, the Royal Canadian Mounted Police (RCMP) released staggering statistics on missing and murdered Indigenous women, girls, and Two Spirit persons, based on police records from across Canada. According to the report, 1,181 Indigenous women are missing or were murdered between 1980 and 2012.[4] However, many advocates and leaders believe this number is closer to 4,000, and it continues to rise.[5]

Leslie Spillett, Knowledge Keeper at Ongomiizwin Indigenous Institute of Health and Healing in Winnipeg, says income insecurity perpetrates violence because it forces Indigenous women, girls, and Two Spirit people into unsafe conditions for survival. This could include gang membership and involvement in the sex industry.

"Economic marginalization really dehumanizes people and when you can dehumanize people, to an extent they become the authors of their own conditions, people get blamed for being in that position. However, the structure that got them there remains intact," she says.

Women involved in the sex industry and women who are victims of human trafficking and sexual exploitation are at higher risk of experiencing violence than other women.[6] The majority of human trafficking victims in Canada are women under 25 years old.[7] Indigenous women, girls, and gender-diverse persons make up the majority of those involved in the street-level sex industry. Many witnesses who shared their stories at the National Inquiry into Missing and Murdered Indigenous Women and Girls (MMIWG) told stories of their missing or murdered loved ones experiencing violence while involved in the sex industry, or as victims of sexual exploitation and human trafficking.[8]

Indigenous Women and the Survival Sex Industry

Alaya McIvor says she could have been a statistic. She was only 12 years old when she was first sexually exploited. "I was in my own home community when it all started. I was put in the care of Child and Family Services [CFS] when I was 12 years old. My CFS worker gave me two ultimatums: either stay in my community at a foster home or go to Winnipeg. I chose the city," she says.

McIvor says her CFS worker bought her a one-way Greyhound bus ticket to Winnipeg and told her to never come back to her community. She says she considers her CFS worker to be her first human trafficker. "I had no idea what to do when I came into the city. No one was there to receive me. There was a lack of communication between my worker and CFS about who was supposed to help me when I got to Winnipeg," she says.

As soon as she arrived in Winnipeg, McIvor says, she was unknowingly lured into sexual exploitation. "There was this man at the Greyhound bus station, which is now considered Balmoral Station in Winnipeg. He picked me up and I acted out his fantasy. I guess some of that was young and dumb, and being naïve in terms of going with that man, but he took advantage of my position at the time. I wasn't getting a lot of support in my community; it's something I was searching for: acceptance," she says.

McIvor says he abandoned her shortly after he abused her: "He tossed me out like a piece of garbage," she says. "He drove me to a Coffee Time on the corner of Princess and Notre Dame, gave me $5, then he drove off. I thought that was normal, so I went back to the station where he lured me." From there she was taken in by sex traffickers and sold across the county.

"My first hit of crack cocaine was at 12 years old. There was nothing for me. Nobody drove up to me on the streets and said, 'Hey, you're a kid, you shouldn't be here.' My peers in the sex industry didn't say that either. We hopped between crack shacks, that's where we lived. They welcome you in with open arms because that's money for them. They know they can benefit off of you," she says. McIvor, now 38, spent more than a decade in the survival sex industry. She says she experienced high levels of violence, poverty, homelessness, and addiction.

"Some of those times were absolutely violent, the acts were just so violent," she says. "I was highly addicted to drugs. I needed to numb the pain from the guy that purchased me and the acts that I just had to play out for him," she says. In 2004, McIvor's best friend, Divas Boulanger, went missing. One month later Boulanger's body was found at a truck stop eight kilometres out of Portage La

Prairie. This sparked McIvor's desire to raise awareness and be a voice for those women and Two Spirit people who died or had gone missing. She now organizes the Annual MMIWG2S (Missing and Murdered Indigenous Women and Girls and Two Spirit) Mother's Day Memorial Walk in Winnipeg, and is a strong advocate for Indigenous women and transgender and Two Spirit communities.

"I wanted to give Divas a voice and I wanted to humanize who she was as an Indigenous trans woman," she says:

> I was determined to move forward in addressing the violence against Indigenous women, and women in general. At that time, I was actively entrenched in my addictions and the sex industry, and I could've at any point in time, on numerous occasions, been one of those statistics of missing or murdered Indigenous women. That always played at the back of my head. Women in the survival sex industry tend to be forgotten about just because they may be addicted, don't have a source of income, and other factors.

There is debate about whether someone's involvement in the sex industry should be considered employment, also referred to as "sex work." Some self-described women's advocate groups believe involvement in the sex industry is a form of exploitation and must be abolished. But many sex-work activist groups believe sex work isn't inherently wrong, that it is in fact useful community work, and that criminalizing it makes women more vulnerable to violence.[9] McIvor prefers using the terminology "survival sex industry," as she believes involvement in the sex industry should not be dignified as "work" but recognized as the exploitation she believes it to be.

A Statistics Canada study found that Indigenous women are 2.7 times more likely to experience violence compared with non-Indigenous women.[10] According to another Statistics Canada study, the differences in victimization rates among Indigenous people is related to a higher presence of other risk factors including lower education levels, childhood maltreatment, unemployment, or being a foster child.[11]

McIvor says that from an Indigenous perspective, based on colonial history and layers of intergenerational trauma, involvement in the sex industry must be seen as a form of exploitation when it involves an Indigenous person: "Our women have been preyed upon for hundreds and hundreds of years; many of them are entrenched in trauma," she says. She recognizes that Indigenous women who are being sexually exploited are at higher risk of going missing or being murdered than non-Indigenous women. Often, Indigenous women are servicing perpetrators outside or in cars, which is more dangerous, she says:

> Indigenous women are put more at risk in the survival sex industry because they're a targeted population. A lot of men know to go to poor communities and exploit those women because no one wants to hear from them, nobody wants to listen to them. These women are seen as less than, they're on the street, they're addicted to drugs. Men know how disadvantaged they are.... If you ask an Indigenous woman what she gets out of working in the survival sex industry, she's not going to say that she's got a house and a car to pay for, she's going to say, "I lost my kids to CFS, I'm an alcoholic." They'll name all of that off. When you ask a non-Indigenous person where they like to work, it'll be at a massage parlour or an indoor space. Indigenous women don't work at massage parlours, they're out on the street. There is no safety for them. Exploitation looks different and opposite for Indigenous women. We're servicing perpetrators in their vehicles, or behind dumpsters. We don't have the luxury of going to a house.

The crisis of missing and murdered Indigenous women and girls and Two Spirit people hit McIvor close to home when, in 2011, her cousin Roberta McIvor was murdered in her home community of Sandy Bay Ojibway First Nation. She was just 32 years old.

The National Inquiry into Missing and Murdered Indigenous Women and Girls

Under mounting public pressure during a federal election in 2015, the newly elected Liberal government launched the National Inquiry into Missing and Murdered Indigenous Women and Girls. The final report, released in 2019, shows how violence is not perpetrated just by the hands of individuals; systems also cause harm.

Colonial systems have been perpetrating violence against Indigenous people through oppressive policies for more than 150 years, according to the Truth and Reconciliation Commission.[12] This includes, but is certainly not limited to, the Indian Act, the residential school system, the outlawing of Indigenous spiritual practices, and the Sixties Scoop.

Leslie Spillett says violence against Indigenous women, girls, and Two Spirit persons is ingrained in Canadian settler-colonial systems:

> When I talk about violence, I don't talk exclusively about domestic violence and violence by individuals. I'm talking about state and structural violence. The colonial project is very integrated in Canadian systems. There is no recognition of this bigger and complex notion that systems are violence at work. Income insecurity is a very large and active act of violence against Indigenous People. The missing and murdered Indigenous women and girls phenomenon you see is the ultimate impact of colonial violence.

The *Final Report* of the National Inquiry into Missing and Murdered Indigenous Women and Girls argues that through its actions and omissions, Canada has been complicit in a genocide against Indigenous women, girls, and gender-diverse persons. The Government of Canada has not publicly agreed with this finding. However, the report states:

> The violence the National Inquiry heard amounts to a race-based genocide of Indigenous Peoples, including First Nations, Inuit, and Métis, which especially targets women, girls, and 2SLGBTQQIA [Two Spirit, lesbian, gay, bisexual, transgender, queer, questioning, intersex, asexual] people. This genocide has been empowered by colonial structures evidenced notably by the Indian Act, the Sixties Scoop, residential schools, and breaches of human and Indigenous rights, leading directly to the current increased rates. The report found that high rates of violence against Indigenous women, Two-Spirit, and gender-diverse people is rooted in systemic factors like economic and social marginalization, racism, discrimination, and misogyny, which are all inherent in Canadian society.[13]

In the National Inquiry's *Final Report*, the commission determined that a basic income could create more economic equality among Canadians and it would be a step towards mitigating violence against Indigenous women and girls and gender-diverse folks. One of the Calls for Justice in the report asks the federal government to: "Establish a guaranteed livable income for all Canadians to ensure equal access to economic and social needs."[14]

Commissioner Qajaq Robinson says personal testimonies that she and fellow commissioners witnessed during the inquiry prompted her to bring forth guaranteed livable income as a recommendation:

> Basic income provides space. Women find themselves in situations of violence where poverty is the reason they can't escape. The focus ends up being how to survive, not to thrive,

> not to heal, not to dream, but to survive.... Indigenous communities are dealing with the legacy of ongoing colonial violence, trauma, economic marginalization, gendered and racialized violence, and violence experienced from institutions.... Our governments have signed onto human rights treaties, conventions, and declarations. We have the means in this country. I think basic income is something that should be applied to all Canadians and society as a whole. I think, though, we have to recognize that special measures are needed for Indigenous peoples to reach substantive equality for there to be true equity.

McIvor says a basic income would move a lot of Indigenous women and transgender and Two Spirit people out of survival mode. "It's just needed, it was needed years ago. Nobody can live off of $200 a month on social assistance. You can't pay a phone bill, hydro bill, cable, and buy groceries off of $200. It keeps our people surviving, meaning they'll do anything to survive. That's where crime comes in," she says. "Basic income is the only way to go to honour our people and give them a sense of dignity."

McIvor says a basic income would have given her the opportunity to heal sooner and create a better life for herself outside of the survival sex industry: "It would've helped a lot when I was entrenched in the survival sex industry. It would have helped me not to pick up more trauma than I did. It would have helped me access healing resources. It would have helped me to not be in a constant survival mode going from one organization to another, trying to eat and trying to live," she says.

Although a basic income is a good step forward, it is not a sufficient solution to the crisis of MMIWG2S in Canada, says Commissioner Robinson. The final report highlighted a total of 231 Calls for Justice to be undertaken by organizations and various levels of government. In 2020, the Native Women's Association of

Canada published a report stating the federal government is failing at implementing the Calls for Justice set forth in the *Final Report*: "This Report Card presents a snapshot of where Canada is situated in relation to the four sets of rights, advanced as part of the National Inquiry's new framework. In the absence of any National Action Plan, it is challenging to award any score other than a resounding 'fail' to the Canadian government."[15]

Despite the national investigation findings and Calls for Justice, the rate at which Indigenous women go missing and are murdered remains the same in Canada, reports CBC News. Between 2016 and 2019, more than 130 Indigenous women and girls were murdered, died suspiciously, or died in institutional care.[16] The prairies have the highest police-reported homicide rate of Indigenous women in Canada, according to 2017 Department of Justice data.[17]

Intimate Partner Violence

Although incidents of violence can be perpetrated by strangers, most of the personal violence against women is as a result of intimate partner violence (IPV). In Canada, according to Statistics Canada, IPV is the leading cause of violence against women and accounts for one-third of all police-reported violent crime.[18] The majority of IPV incidents occurs in private homes. A study from Canada's Department of Justice shows that self-reported spousal violence of Indigenous women is three times higher than that of non-Indigenous women in Canada.[19]

Manitoba has the highest rate of femicide among provinces, according to the latest report by the Canadian Femicide Observatory for Justice and Accountability.[20] Statistics Canada says Manitoba is also leading in police-reported intimate partner violence with the second-highest rate in Canada, followed by Saskatchewan.[21]

Deena Brock, the provincial coordinator at Manitoba Association of Women's Shelters, says that despite high rates of IPV in the province, many women still aren't able to identify if they're in an abusive situation, which suggests that the rate is likely much higher than reported. "A lot of women underestimate the level of risk that they are experiencing or they don't consider it abuse because maybe they've lived with it all their lives," says Brock. "They may have even seen their mom in this situation, so that's normal to them. A lot of times we get these calls and women will say, 'Well, I'm not being abused, but I'm feeling uncomfortable.'"

However, most abused women are not passive victims. Research from the World Health Organization suggests women adapt coping strategies in order to maintain safety for their children.[22] The reasons women stay in a violent relationship include fear of retaliation, economic instability, concern for children's safety, and lack of a support network, among others.[23]

One of the biggest reasons women stay in violent situations is because poverty, or lack of financial independence, limits their ability to leave. Brock says that regardless of socio-economic status, some women don't even have access to their own bank accounts because they're controlled by their partner. "Money's probably one of the biggest fears," says Brock. "You can't rent an apartment and you can't purchase bus tickets. If you don't have money, you can't get away from him. It's a huge issue. This gets brought up often on the crisis line: I don't have money, I don't have a credit card, I don't have ID."

Lisa Carriere, the community support manager at the North End Women's Centre, agrees. Income insecurity and lack of identification holds many women back from leaving an abusive relationship. "A lot of times there are financial issues. That's a really big barrier. For example, if a woman is working, she doesn't necessarily have access to her own money in the relationship. Sometimes they don't have ID, [and] finding safe and affordable housing is very challenging, especially if you're on a lower income." Brock says many of the women who access women's shelters in Manitoba are on provincial social assistance, and accessing the labour market is challenging.

Trauma and its Impact on Women Seeking Employment

Women who have experienced trauma and have left an abusive situation have immense barriers to entering, or re-entering, the workforce, according to author Linda DeRiviere. In *The Healing Journey*, DeRiviere recounts how women leave abusive unions only to find themselves in working poverty. Ongoing emotional and physical abuse by a partner can have detrimental impacts on a woman's ability to earn an education, and can negatively impact her workforce goals.[24] Social assistance programs have policies that create further barriers to adequate employment and leave many women in poverty. Women and gender-diverse people who have left an abusive situation may not be ready for the work-readiness standards of welfare programs. DeRiviere states:

> While a transitional period of reliance on welfare assistance is an important safety net, it can also keep women trapped in poverty and, in some situations, perpetuate the cycle of violence…. The notion that putting fixed limits on welfare duration will result in self-sufficiency for women who would be holding down well-paid jobs is not one that works for many women. In fact it could lead to more "dangerous dependencies," as some women return to an abuser or start another abuse relationship to survive. Other women may join in sex trade and/or other informal labour market activities in order to obtain money to feed their family.[25]

Carriere says despite provincial assistance's being a "social safety net," income levels are well below the poverty line: "Women can't afford to rent an apartment, if they can it's a rundown hole. Many women are staying in rooming houses that are terrible and not well taken care of. Plus, rooming houses often have … violence," she says. "Social assistance is not anywhere close to being sufficient and this forces some women into sex work, or they'll stay with someone they don't know for a while just to have a place to stay. It really does become about survival."

Child care is also a major barrier to women's ability to obtain and maintain employment. Women perform two-thirds of unpaid caregiving, which can significantly reduce their ability to participate fully in the paid labour market.[26] Accessible and affordable child care remains a problem across Canada. Many mothers are forced to choose between paid work and child care.

Basic Income and the Canada Child Benefit Are Necessary Safety Nets

Many experts working in the field of domestic violence recognize how crucial the Canada Child Benefit (CCB) is for mothers leaving an abusive relationship. The CCB is a form of basic income for families with children under 18 years old. Parents receive a predictable amount of money every month, based solely on their income and the child's age. This can be used however a parent wants to use it.

Carriere says the extra money gives mothers a lot more financial freedom. "It's absolutely important to have that Canada Child Benefit. It gives so much more room for these women. If you're on Employment and Income Assistance you only have a small amount that you can pay for rent. You can top that up with the money you get from the Canada Child Benefit and live in a safer neighbourhood," she says. "Once you pay your rent and pay your bills, often there's not a lot of money left, if any. It can also help with buying groceries, clothes, and extras for the family. That could even mean the difference between buying cable or buying a phone."

Angela Braun, the executive director of Genesis House, a women's shelter in rural Manitoba, says a basic income would create a sense of stability in the lives of domestic abuse survivors: "It would reduce the level of stress. Knowing that there is going to be that safety net, knowing how much it's going to be, knowing that it's not going to vary month to month, it would really reduce a lot of stress," says Braun. "[Women] would be able to properly plan and budget. If there is not enough in the budget to cover all of the basic expenses, you can budget until the cows come home, but there's still not enough money there."

She says the Canada Child Benefit is a good example of how women benefit from a guaranteed income. "People wondered if recipients of the CCB would drink it away, or waste it. That's not what we've seen. We've seen that women are not needing to find social housing and choosing to use that money to buy market housing. Women are better off on the Canada Child Benefit than on provincial income assistance. We're very quick to judge how these women are going to choose to spend the money," says Braun. Basic income, like the CCB, would help women to access better housing, to plan, and to budget.

However, family dynamics can be challenging. In an abusive relationship, income is often controlled by a male partner, says Deena Brock. "If a woman is in a relationship and getting a basic income, most of them won't see it because he will control it," she says. "He'll love it, but it won't help the woman or the children."

Braun agrees that income could be used as a manipulation tactic: "If the man knew she had the money, then he would just force her to give it up. Even if she wasn't physically forced to give it up, morally, she has been taught that her husband calls the shots so she couldn't withhold that money from him," she says.

Author Mary Ellsberg and others study results from cash transfer programs in developing nations, which show that in fact stipends could reduce the level of violence women experience at home. An article in *The Lancet* by Ellsberg et al. says, "Studies around the world have consistently shown associations between intimate partner violence and poverty at both a household and community level ... increasing ... women's economic opportunities should be a key strategy to reduce violence ... cash transfer programmes can contribute to reductions in both intimate partner violence and child marriage."[27] A cash transfer study conducted in Kenya linked women's economic independence with an increase in female empowerment and improved psychological well-being.[28]

Basic income is not the sole solution to abuse. Other supports, like those offered at women's shelters, are needed to ensure the safety of women and children. However, a basic income could provide women with more financial freedom to choose their own path to independence.

References

[1] Phumzile Mlambo-Ngcuka, "Violence against Women and Girls: The Shadow Pandemic," *UN Women* (2000), https://www.unwomen.org/en/news/stories/2020/4/statement-ed-phumzile-violence-against-women-during-pandemic

[2] Statistics Canada, *Canadians Living in Low-Income Households Experience Higher Rates of Violent Victimization*, 2015, https://www150.statcan.gc.ca/n1/pub/85f0033m/2009020/findings-resultats/f-r2-eng.htm#n1

[3] Government of Canada, *Breaking the Links between Poverty and Violence against Women: A Resource Guide—The Reality of Poverty and Violence*, 2012, https://www.canada.ca/en/public-health/services/health-promotion/stop-family-violence/prevention-resource-centre/women/violence-against-women-resource-guide/reality-poverty-violence.html

[4] Royal Canadian Mounted Police, *Missing and Murdered Aboriginal Women: A National Operational Overview*, 2014, 3, http://www.mmiwg-ffada.ca/wp-content/uploads/2018/04/national-operational-overview.pdf

[5] John Paul Tasker, "Confusion Reigns over Number of Missing, Murdered Indigenous Women," CBC News, February 16, 2016, https://www.cbc.ca/news/politics/mmiw-4000-hajdu-1.3450237

[6] National Inquiry into Missing and Murdered Indigenous Women and Girls (MMIWG), *Reclaiming Power and Place: The Final Report of the National Inquiry into Missing and Murdered Indigenous Women and Girls*, 2019, vol. 1a, 656, https://www.mmiwg-ffada.ca/wp-content/uploads/2019/06/Final_Report_Vol_1a-1.pdf

[7] Statistics Canada, *Trafficking in Persons in Canada*, 2016, https://www150.statcan.gc.ca/n1/daily-quotidien/180627/dq180627g-eng.htm

[8] MMIWG, 656.

[9] Ibid.

[10] Statistics Canada, *Study: Women in Canada: Women and the Criminal Justice System*, 2017, https://www150.statcan.gc.ca/n1/daily-quotidien/170606/dq170606a-eng.htm

[11] Statistics Canada, *Victimization of Aboriginal people in Canada*, 2014, https://www150.statcan.gc.ca/n1/pub/85-002-x/2016001/article/14631-eng.htm

[12] Truth and Reconciliation Commission of Canada (TRC), *Honouring the Truth, Reconciling for the Future: Summary of the Final Report of the Truth and Reconciliation Commission of Canada*, 2015, http://nctr.ca/assets/reports/Final%20Reports/Executive_Summary_English_Web.pdf

[13] MMIWG, 50.

[14] MMIWG, 182.

[15] Native Women's Assocation of Canada, *Report Card on Government Follow-Up to Reclaiming Power and Place: Final Report of the National Inquiry into Missing and Murdered Indigenous Women and Girls*, 2020, 3, https://www.nwac.ca/wp-content/uploads/2020/06/REPORT-CARD.pdf

[16] Jorge Barerra, "MMIWG Cases Continued at Same Rate Even after National Inquiry Began, Data Shows," CBC News, June 5, 2019, https://www.cbc.ca/news/indigenous/mmiwg-inquiry-new-cases-statistics-databases-1.5162482

[17] Canada, Department of Justice, "JustFacts: Missing and Murdered Indigenous Women and Girls," July 2017, https://www.justice.gc.ca/eng/rp-pr/jr/jf-pf/2017/july04.html

[18] Statistics Canada, *Family Violence in Canada: A Statistical Profile*, 2018, https://www150.statcan.gc.ca/n1/pub/85-002-x/2019001/article/00018/02-eng.htm

[19] Canada, Department of Justice, "JustFacts: Victimization of Indigenous Women and Girls," July 2017, https://www.justice.gc.ca/eng/rp-pr/jr/jf-pf/2017/july05.html

[20] Canadian Femicide Observatory for Justice and Accountability, *#Callitfemicide: Understanding Gender-Related Killings of Women and Girls in Canada 2019*, 2019, 7, https://femicideincanada.ca/callitfemicide2019.pdf

[21] Statistics Canada, *Section 2: Police-Reported Intimate Partner Violence in Canada*, 2018,

https://www150.statcan.gc.ca/n1/pub/85-002-x/2019001/article/00018/02-eng.htm

[22] World Health Organization, *Understanding and Addressing Violence against Women*, 2012, 3, https://apps.who.int/iris/bitstream/handle/10665/77432/WHO_RHR_12.36_eng.pdf?sequence=1

[23] Ibid.

[24] Linda DeRiviere, *The Healing Journey: Intimate Partner Violence and Its Impacts on the Labour Market* (Winnipeg: Fernwood Publishing, 2014), 43.

[25] Ibid., 62–99.

[26] Colleen Reid and Robin LeDrew, "The Burden of Being 'Employable': Underpaid and Unpaid Work and Women's Health," *Journal of Women and Social Work* 28, no. 1 (February 2013): 81.

[27] Mary Ellsberg, Diana Arango, Matthew Morton, Floriza Gennari, Sveinung Kiplesund, Manuel Contreras, and Charlotte Watts, "Prevention of Violence against Women and Girls: What Does the Evidence Say?" *The Lancet* 385 (November 2014): 1563, http://bibliobase.sermais.pt:8008/BiblioNET/Upload/PDF10/007705%20PIIS0140-6736(14)61703-7.pdf

[28] Johannes Haushofer and Jeremy Shapiro, "Household Response to Income Changes: Evidence from an Unconditional Cash Transfer Program in Kenya," 2013, 36, https://www.poverty-action.org/sites/default/files/publications/Haushofer_Shapiro_UCT_2013.pdf

8

Basic Income, Reconciliation, and the Way Forward

One theme that has reverberated throughout this book is poverty: poverty as a predictable catalyst, consequence, and ubiquitous presence for some who live complicated lives. Who is living below the poverty line in Canada?

Some people are more likely to live with poverty than others. People between the ages of 45 and 64 who are living alone face the greatest depth of poverty in Canada, and those aged 65 and above are least likely to be living in deep poverty. Despite the Canada Child Benefit, too many children under 18 who are living with a single parent, especially a single mother, still live with poverty. Inuit, Métis, and especially First Nations people are more likely to have incomes below the poverty line, and the risk increases dramatically for those who live on-reserve or in remote areas of the country. Racialized people have a higher incidence of poverty than other Canadians. People with disabilities are among the poorest people in Canada. Women are more likely to live in poverty than are men.[1]

Social programs in Canada are comparatively generous for those 65 and over who have access to Old Age Security (OAS) and, if they lack a pension from the Canada or Quebec Pension Plans or private sources, the Guaranteed Income Supplement. Despite this, many seniors still experience poverty. Families with children have a lower incidence of poverty than adults living alone because the Canada Child Benefit helps to lift many, but not all, above the poverty line.

Social programs have been less generous towards adults of working age, who are expected to support themselves by working for a wage. As a consequence, the provincial income assistance programs that provide support for this age group are programs of last resort that offer meagre support only when an applicant can demonstrate virtual destitution. Working-age people with disabilities, even when they cannot work, fare little better.

Indigenous people, whether they live on-reserve or elsewhere, bear an additional burden. On a reserve, funding for basic social services such as health care, child welfare, education, and more falls well below the levels offered elsewhere in the country. Basic infrastructure, such as water and sewage, is often inadequate. Substandard housing is common. All of these factors are the result of conscious political decisions that held funding for reserves below the rates of population growth and inflation for decades. Residential schools and the Sixties Scoop are only two manifestations of an ongoing colonial legacy that undermines Indigenous sovereignty, ceremony, and culture, and continues to affect Indigenous people wherever they live.

Poverty is complex, and there is no single intervention that will address an issue that has in many cases been generations in the making. People who have the ability to work but lack job skills need dedicated programs that will provide those skills. People who use substances need access to safe consumption sites, to supportive housing, and to addiction treatment programs. People with disabilities need dedicated supports, whether these take the form of assistive devices, pharmaceuticals, medical care, supportive housing, or other supports needed to succeed in education and the workplace. People in abusive relationships need access to emergency shelters and dedicated programming. Notably, many people have multiple needs that interact with one another.

None of these supports is adequate on its own. People also need access to a basic income sufficient to live with dignity and a sense of independence and security. A basic income paid in the form of money rather than services gives people the autonomy to make their own decisions about how to live their own lives. It is not a substitute for good medical care or an adequate educational system. It is, however, the way in which someone can choose for themselves whether they need more education or simply time away from the demands of work to process a difficult life transition. It would allow, for example, a rural resident to pay a friend or neighbour for a ride into town when there is no public transportation; a person in an abusive relationship to buy a bus ticket so they could leave; or a friend to share resources with someone they know who is going through a difficult time.

The Dimensions of a Basic Income

These values are at the heart of what makes a basic income different from provincial income assistance.

1. Basic income is **unconditional**. The amount received does not depend on the discretion of a caseworker or the behaviour of the applicant.

2. Basic income is **adequate**. The guarantee is set at a level that would not force an applicant to live with an income far below the poverty line.

3. Basic income is **guaranteed**. The amount received is predictable; it depends only on the other income an individual has. Its predictability allows people to plan their lives.

4. Basic income is **responsive**. It responds to changing income levels and family circumstances in a timely way.

5. Basic income is delivered with **dignity and respect**. No one should be forced to reveal details of their personal lives or their relationships with others. No one should be required to submit to drug tests, or to attend twelve-step programs or training programs as a condition of support.
6. Basic income respects individual **autonomy**. No one should be required to produce receipts to demonstrate what they spend money on.

The purpose of a basic income is to ensure that no one in Canada is forced to live below the poverty line. A basic income guarantee is income-tested, in the sense that someone with no other income receives the full benefit set at a level close to the poverty line. Those who work and receive a wage but still do not earn enough to live above the poverty line would receive an amount reduced by some portion of their other income. This structure means that people who earn an income just above the poverty line still receive a partial benefit. The basic income would be gradually reduced as other sources of income increase until, at higher incomes, it falls to zero. The amount received from the government is based only on the amount of other income, so anyone can easily calculate how much they are entitled to receive.

By contrast, people who today rely on provincial income or disability support face a bewildering array of different benefit levels and special allowances in every province. A sympathetic caseworker might find extra resources for a client, while a different caseworker will not offer additional help to another client in a very similar situation. Sometimes clients receive extra help only if they know to ask for it. Sometimes clients learn about special benefits only from online groups or by overhearing conversations in clinics or waiting rooms. Many food banks and health-care clinics that serve low-income populations hire people to help clients access the benefits to which they are entitled. These programs are supplemented by a set of federal and provincial tax credits for low-income people, but many low-income people don't file tax returns: because their incomes are so low, they don't have to pay taxes.[2] However, by not filing taxes, they forego benefits they would otherwise receive, such as the GST Rebate, the Canada Workers Benefit, and, in some cases, provincial tax credits.

The existing set of income supports for low-income people is far from guaranteed and predictable. It requires low-income people to file federal and provincial tax returns, which they are not required by law to do. Provincial benefits vary depending on what an applicant knows to ask for and on how sympathetic a caseworker might be. By contrast, a basic income would consolidate many of these monetary benefits into a single higher amount based on other income, so that everyone in similar circumstances would receive the same amount of support.

Basic income must also be able to respond to changing circumstances, which means that it should be easy to apply for and quick to arrive. We all learned many things about ourselves and our society when the COVID-19 pandemic caused public health officials to shut down large tracts of the economy. One of the things we learned was, when necessity calls, civil servants can transform the way social programs are delivered. When working people lost their jobs, policy-makers recognized very quickly that Employment Insurance was inadequate to meet the needs of so many people out of work at one time. The government responded by creating the Canada Emergency Response Benefit (CERB) that paid $2,000 a month to displaced workers—more than twice what an adult living alone can expect to receive from provincial income assistance.

The most significant thing we learned, however, was not about how to design an emergency program but rather about how to administer one. Within a couple of weeks of the shutdown, it was decided to deliver the CERB through online accounts that are used by many Canadians to pay their income tax. An applicant could easily complete a simplified application form online, state their income, and submit the form. Within days, the CERB money arrived directly into the applicant's bank account. Those without online accounts could set one up quickly, and people without Internet access or those who needed additional support had a telephone number to call an administrator who would complete the form on their behalf. No one had to have filed a tax return in order to be eligible, and the amount of money they received depended only on current monthly income. This delivery method was made possible by a simple directive to administrators, who were told to pay the money to applicants and wait to confirm eligibility until after the applicant's work life had stabilized. That is, they were told to trust the applicant first, then to verify the claim.

The experience of CERB applicants is remarkable because it is so very different from applying for provincial income assistance. Income assistance requires a visit to a caseworker, with vast amounts of paperwork, and, importantly, no money changes hands until the documentation is checked out and eligibility confirmed. Every statement is verified with banks, landlords and other agencies, and the relationships between all household residents are documented. Applicants are required to apply for any other support to which they might be entitled, and will not receive any money from provincial income assistance until other resources are exhausted. There are strict asset limits, which mean that savings will be drained before income assistance is offered. An applicant is required to follow a plan designed to find employment. In some cases, this means submitting a certain number of résumés each month or attending job readiness training. If an applicant does not comply, the claim may be denied. Applicants are required to supply any documentation requested, whenever it is requested, at risk of claim denial. If the application is successful, the amount of money an applicant receives depends on other income, their documented needs, and on the discretion of a caseworker who might offer or deny additional benefits based on particular circumstances.

If basic income were delivered in the same way that the CERB was delivered, it would be simple to apply for and responsive to changing needs. The amount received would be predictable and reliable. The application process would respect the dignity, privacy, and autonomy of applicants. Most important, the amount would be adequate to live with dignity in a high-income country like Canada.

Why Don't We Have a Basic Income?

The need for a basic income is obvious. No amount of tinkering can transform the existing social safety net in Canada into a system that respects the dignity and autonomy of recipients and offers a predictable income sufficient to meet modest needs. The opposition to basic income falls into two distinct categories: paternalism—which encompasses racial, gender, and other biases—and cost.

"Paternalism" is the belief that people who need financial assistance cannot be trusted to make their own decisions, either because they will harm themselves or take advantage of others. This is what lies behind the work requirements, invasive needs-testing, surveillance, and monitoring of the existing income assistance system. However, there have been basic income experiments all over the world, in low-, middle-, and high-income countries, and the one thing that emerges time after time is that people with a basic income are capable of articulating their own needs and making decisions to meet those needs. Even if that weren't the case, everyone has the fundamental right to identify their own needs and to make their own decisions. There is no evidence that people who apply for income assistance are less honest than anybody else. In sheer dollar terms, tax fraud by high-income individuals certainly vastly eclipses welfare fraud by those with low incomes. In Ontario, corporate crime, white-collar fraud, and tax evasion cost the public more every year than the entire cost of the social assistance system.[3] A study by the Parliamentary Budget Office (PBO), which is the arm's-length body charged with the task of estimating the costs of federal budgets, shows that in 2019, provinces and territories collectively spent about $20 billion delivering income assistance to people living in poverty; in the same year, Canada lost $25 billion in tax revenue through illegal tax evasion by corporations and mostly high-income individuals and an additional $24 billion through aggressive tax avoidance by corporations that use legal tax loopholes.[4] Yet there is far more public outrage about a single mom charged with welfare fraud than about a high-flying executive charged with tax evasion. The hardest barrier to overcome is the implicit belief that, despite all the evidence to the contrary, those who have done relatively well financially are both smarter and more honest than those with fewer resources.

Sometimes paternalism is openly harsh, as in the case of work requirements: "these people should learn the value of working hard like I do!" Other times, it takes a deceptively benevolent veneer, as in the argument that "we must be sure that we do not cause harm to recipients by, for example, giving resources to people with substance use issues. Do we want to be responsible for more opioid deaths?" Paternalism is often the unspoken justification for alternatives offered to basic income, such as "guaranteed jobs" or "guaranteed services." Guaranteed jobs would force people to work in order to receive the resources they need to live, usually justified by the claim that work is good for people. In fact, working *is* good for people, and we know most people agree because of how hard they try to find a job when they don't have one, but not everyone can work. Some people find self-esteem and meaning in life from the work they are paid to do. However, there are many other people who find their real purpose in life outside the paid labour market—people who provide unpaid care for other family members, artists and creators, volunteers, and others. Still others need time to themselves to heal from a lifetime of trauma before they are in any position to look for work.

Similarly, guaranteed services would decide what it is people really need rather than letting them decide for themselves. Paternalism is also the motivation for the argument that a basic income would make people with disabilities worse off, suggesting against all evidence that the current system actually provides people with disabilities with the supports and services they need, and that only with the help of a caseworker can they be assured that their needs are met.

When government policy takes the form of public services, it provides those services in a manner consistent with the expectations of the majority. As a consequence, public health care has a dismal record of meeting the needs of Black and Indigenous peoples, and people of colour, as well as gender-nonconforming people. The overpolicing of Black and Indigenous communities is another example. Government paternalism reflects all of the race, gender, disability, and cultural biases that have been examined throughout this book. As well, policy is designed, implemented, and evaluated by members of the dominant culture and also reflects its implicit biases. It meets the needs of those who conform to cultural norms, but the more one deviates from those categories of favour, the less adequately one's specific needs are met by those policies.

Needless to say, neither providing jobs nor ensuring access to necessary services is a bad thing; in fact, basic income complements a well-functioning labour market and good public services. But we still need money that we can spend to meet our own unique needs as well as the needs others have identified for us.

If people have the money they need and the freedom to allocate that money any way they like, they have the capacity to free themselves from coercive social structures. The power relationships cemented into public policy and enacted through bureaucracies, caseworkers, and government-appointed experts are undermined. Paternalism undervalues the lives of those involved in the sex industry, people who use substances, racialized people, people with disabilities, and many others. Basic income allows people to escape paternalism and to meet their own needs in the ways they believe best.

The other objection to basic income is that it simply costs too much. There have been several studies that estimate the cost of a guaranteed basic income, some of which were conducted by the Parliamentary Budget Office. In 2020, the PBO estimated what a basic income would cost in the context of the COVID-19 pandemic.[5] The PBO offered some very large numbers, but the takeaway message was that, however expensive it would be to offer a basic income in the context of a pandemic, it would still cost less than alternatives such as tinkering with Employment Insurance so that more people would qualify for higher payments and continuing the CERB. Any system would cost a lot in a year when more people than usual are out of work or on short hours because of a pandemic.

In fact, one of the benefits of a basic income is that it automatically expands during harsh economic times and contracts when the economy is doing well and fewer people are out of work. That automatic adjustment is its chief strength, because it ensures that people have what they need when they need it, to support themselves and their families.

If we want to know whether we can afford a basic income, it is more helpful to estimate its costs during normal economic times, which the PBO did in 2021.[6] They noted that the federal government and the provinces already deliver cash to low-income individuals and families through dozens of different programs, with different application procedures, different eligibility requirements and different regulations, but these programs are so ineffective that 8.7 per cent of the population still lives below the poverty line. Others have noted that the bureaucracies governing these programs are so complex that many do not receive the benefits to which they are entitled.[7] The PBO showed that by streamlining and enhancing cash transfers through a basic income, they could substantially increase the amount of money received by recipients of provincial income assistance and cut the rate of poverty in Canada by 49 per cent. They could replace ineffective cash transfers by a basic income without increasing tax rates, imposing new taxes or eliminating programs that deliver services for particular needs such as disability supports. Transitioning to a basic income is challenging, but Canada clearly has the financial capacity to offer a basic income. Basic income is an investment in our communities. If we offer all residents of Canada a basic income, we gain a return on that investment in the form of healthy people, healthy families, and healthy communities. Make no mistake: poverty is expensive and we already pay its costs in the form of elevated health-care costs, costs for shelters, and higher education costs, at the same time that the criminalization of poverty results in money being poured into ever-increasing policing and criminal justice costs. We wait for people to get sick and then we treat the consequences of their poverty in our health-care system; we wait for children living with poverty to struggle in school and then we devise special education programs and social supports to address the consequences of their poverty; we criminalize disadvantaged youth and lead them down a school-to-prison pipeline in a massively funded system of incarceration. Doesn't it make sense to offer a little more money upfront so that people can live better lives?

Contributing to Reconciliation

The principles on which basic income is based, specifically autonomy and respect, should govern the relations not only between individual residents of Canada and the government but also between the provinces and the federal government, and, especially, between the federal government and Indigenous communities.

Canada has an established system that allows provinces to deliver national programs with compensation from the federal government as long as they offer their residents a program that meets the national government standard. For example, Quebec runs its own counterpart to the Canada Pension Plan. A similar system could support the delivery of a national basic income while respecting provincial autonomy.

However, the federal government can provide leadership by offering a basic income without infringing on provincial autonomy even without this mechanism. If the federal government were to create a basic income, delivered through online accounts on a monthly basis just as the CERB was delivered, provinces would be free to respond as they like. The federal government could exempt provincial income assistance payments from the calculation of income for the purposes of basic income, and any province that wanted to continue to offer provincial income assistance in addition to the federal basic income would be free to do so. The more likely result is that provinces would reduce their provincial income assistance by the amount of the federal basic income. Basic income would effectively make everyone ineligible for provincial income assistance. Since basic income would be higher than provincial income assistance, recipients would be better off.

Provinces, too, would be better off and could reallocate some of that money no longer required for income assistance to other expenditures like additional supportive housing, health care, long-term care, education, and additional services for people with disabilities. The choice of how to reallocate would remain with each province.

One important step is acknowledging the legitimate will and capacity of First Nations communities to make their own decisions—something this country has failed at. Indigenous people have figured heavily in this book because Indigenous people are much more likely to be living in poverty than other residents of Canada. How can we ensure that Indigenous communities are well served by a basic income?

Approximately 5 per cent of the Canadian population identifies as Indigenous—First Nations, non-Status, Métis, or Inuit. About half of registered First Nations people with Status live on-reserve or in First Nations communities. The overwhelming majority of non-Status Indigenous people and Métis live in urban areas. According to the 2016 Census, the average total income of an Indigenous person was 75 per cent of that of a non-Indigenous person, and that of a First Nations person was 66 per cent that of a non-Indigenous person. First Nations children were twice as likely to live in poverty as other children.[7]

For people living off-reserve, basic income provides the same benefits as it does for other residents of Canada: income support through life transitions and insurance against the unforeseen. It provides a bit of extra space to think about investing in education or starting a new business, and the security of knowing there is enough money to pay the rent and put food on the table. For Indigenous communities, however, there are additional factors to consider.

Housing, education, health care, and food security are pressing issues in many First Nations communities, and a basic income is no substitute for programs designed to ensure that people living on-reserve have access to the same public services as people living elsewhere in Canada. Basic infrastructure, such as clean drinking water and waste-water arrangements, which are sorely lacking in many communities, should be a given for all people in a high-income country like Canada. Basic income is not a substitute. Many reserves share with other rural and remote communities the absence of broadband Internet service. Even basic bus service is unavailable in many parts of rural Canada, and the costs of flying are exorbitant. Some communities are fly-in only or have road access only during winter. Basic income alone is not anywhere close to what is required to sufficiently meet all the needs of First Nations communities, and should not be used as a substitute for providing the investments necessary to improve living conditions on-reserve.

Particularly in the North, the cost of living is very much higher than elsewhere in Canada. It would be extremely complex and not terribly efficient to have a different basic income for every small community; it is much more reasonable to imagine basic income as a floor, and to recognize that other policies are necessary to deal with particular local needs. Food security in the North, for example, requires solutions to deal with the high costs of transportation in addition to a basic income that allows people to define and meet their own needs.

What should a basic income on-reserve look like, and how should it be administered? Just as provincial income assistance deprives applicants of respect and autonomy, the Government of Canada has a long tradition of depriving First Nations communities of respect and autonomy. Traditionally, First Nations were provided with direct services that were designed and controlled by Ottawa. To the extent that funding was provided directly to First Nations communities, it was constrained by so many reports to different agencies of the federal government that band offices were overwhelmed. Communities were not afforded the respect and freedom to make their own social and financial decisions. More recently, there have been painfully slow attempts to devolve some control to First Nations in policy areas such as health care, child welfare, and education, but progress has been glacial.

The role of the federal government should be to provide funding but to leave decision-making authority with communities. Indigenous governments are perfectly capable of deciding what they need for themselves. The federal government should be a willing but a non-controlling partner. The design of a basic income on-reserve is an opportunity to respect Indigenous sovereignty. If Indigenous communities decide that a basic income is an appropriate policy, the federal government should be a willing partner. If they decide that a basic income is not appropriate, the federal government should not impose one. Indigenous communities should have the right to opt out, with a guarantee that per capita funding equivalent to the national basic income would be provided for whatever system is ultimately created, along with assistance and funding to build administrative capacity.

Income assistance on-reserve has traditionally been funded by the federal government, often in partnership with or under contract to the provinces. The amount of funding received by someone on-reserve was set by the province in which it is situated. However, many people on-reserve live in subsidized housing, so the amount received is usually only the "basic needs" portion of provincial income assistance—typically slightly less than half the amount received by someone not living in subsidized housing.

A government evaluation of the On-Reserve Income Assistance Program was published in 2018.[8] As a consequence of that report, there is a commitment from the federal government to engage in a five-year negotiation with stakeholders to co-develop and implement changes and improvements to the program. That platform could allow First Nations to engage in the development of a culturally appropriate basic income, which might, in the end, look very different from a basic income delivered elsewhere in the country. The decision, ultimately, must rest with First Nations themselves.

It Took a Pandemic to Show Us That We Are All Connected

Canadian society puts a high value on the hard work and contributions of individuals. Some people resent any suggestion that their lifestyle is based on privilege when they consider how hard they have worked to earn what they have. If we imagine society as a collection of individuals, then a greater share going to some, however hard they might work, means less for others. Basic income is a proposal to share the benefits of economic growth with people who have traditionally been left out: people with disabilities, low-income workers, young adults aging out of care, people who devote their time to caring for others rather than working for pay, people with mental health challenges and substance use issues, people leaving institutions, and others who are consistently left at the margins of society. Such a proposal is bound to be resisted by some taxpayers.

However, during the COVID-19 pandemic we were forced to recognize that our communities are much more than collections of individuals. We couldn't fail to see that our own health depends on the health of everyone else. When some front-line workers had no access to sick leave, they had no choice but to work and put their co-workers at risk, even if they experienced symptoms of COVID-19. When low wages forced personal care workers to work at many different long-term care homes with too little time and inadequate resources for safety procedures, they became a vector for infection. When pandemic fears and supply-chain issues challenged food banks, people who relied on income assistance and disability support went without food. People with other health issues found themselves without the medical care they needed as resources were shifted to victims of the pandemic. It's clear that the physical health of any one of us depends on the health of others.

It is less apparent, but no less real, that our economic health depends on the economic well-being of others. As the economy reopened, the small businesses that survived did so only because their customers had income that they could spend. Had it not been for emergency income supports like the CERB, the economic consequences of the pandemic would have been much worse as the income losses associated with one bankruptcy led to further income losses that put other firms in jeopardy. Those with the most precarious earnings would bear a disproportionate burden as they would be hit first and hardest by economic closures, but the devastation would ultimately spread to everyone as firm after firm succumbed.

When elementary schools were closed and learning shifted online, existing inequalities were exacerbated. Some children struggled to learn in inadequate space with less than reliable computer equipment and Internet access while others shared resources in spaces dedicated to their education. Some high school and university students coped with online learning while others, particularly those with many challenges in their lives, could not continue. These educational interruptions will have repercussions that will last for decades, and they will fall disproportionately on those already struggling. However, everyone, not just those hit hardest, will bear the consequences of these disruptions. It has been estimated that students in grades one through twelve will earn 3 per cent less income over their lifetimes because of learning disruptions, and economic growth will be reduced by 1.5 per cent each year for the rest of the century.[9]

The pandemic made us recognize our interdependence, but that interdependence is not just an artifact of the pandemic. Even before COVID-19, we bore the burden of the poverty and inequality that existed in our society even if we were not, ourselves, living in poverty. There is not a single social problem that is not exacerbated by poverty, as the stories in this book have made clear. We are all affected in different ways by the struggles of people without adequate housing, even when we do not live on the streets ourselves. We all are affected by poverty-related crime, even if we are not poor. We are all affected by the poverty and poor health of our neighbours. The moral burden of inequality should be obvious to us all, and we are all affected by the economic burden as well.

It took a pandemic to show us that we are all connected. The physical health of one of us affects us all. The mental health of one of us affects us all. The economic health of one of us affects us all.

Next Steps

For decades, our social safety net has been fraying and the economy has been changing. Until now, we have paid for the over-policing of some of our neighbours and the institutionalization of others, instead of ensuring that our relatives and neighbours have the resources to live. We have paid for the consequences of poverty through our hospital emergency departments, and the consequences of child poverty through our educational system. The pandemic was the shock that drove the message home. We need a better, simpler, more adequate method of addressing persistent poverty and ensuring financial security for all people in Canada. It is possible to transform the Canadian social safety net, recognizing the strength and capacity of individuals to decide how to live their own lives. It is possible to act as a willing and responsive partner, making resources available to people without coercing them to behave in particular ways or punishing them for non-compliance.

However, the path is challenging. The barriers imposed by paternalism haven't disappeared in the wake of the pandemic, and the voices of austerity are growing louder as the cost of dealing with the pandemic becomes clearer. It is, for that reason, heartening to observe that support for basic income is also growing.

As the pandemic rolled out across Canada in successive waves, more and more people began to recognize that the way we had been doing things for many years was simply no longer adequate. Basic income always had strong support among social welfare advocates, disability rights activists, social workers, and the health-care community—groups that traditionally recognized our interdependence. Indigenous women offered leadership through the *Final Report* of the National Inquiry into Missing and Murdered Indigenous Women and Girls. But as the pandemic unfolded, new voices from across the political spectrum joined the traditional supporters of basic income: the Steelworkers Union, the Canadian Chamber of Commerce, the Synod of Anglican Bishops, the Pope, the United Church, more than 4,000 individual women and women's groups, organizations representing more than 70,000 artists, and many others. They shared little beyond the recognition that basic income makes us all better off, and is something well worth fighting for.

References

[1] Evelyn L. Forget, *Basic Income for Canadians: From the COVID-19 Emergency to Financial Security for All* (Toronto: Lorimer and Co., 2020), 32–33, 136ff.

[2] Jennifer Robson and Saul Schwartz, "Who Doesn't File a Tax Return? A Portrait of Non-filers," *Canadian Public Policy* 46, No. 3 (September 2020): 323–39.

[3] Canada, Department of Justice, *Six Degrees from Liberation: Legal Needs of Women in Criminal and Other Matters*, 2015, https://www.justice.gc.ca/eng/rp-pr/csj-sjc/jsp-sjp/rr03_la20-rr03_aj20/p3.html

[4] Parliamentary Budget Office, "Preliminary Findings on International Taxation," June 20, 2019. https://www.pbo-dpb.gc.ca/en/blog/news/preliminary-findings-on-international-taxation

[5] Nasreddine Ammar, Carleigh Malanik-Busby, and Salma Mohamed Ahmed, "Costing a Basic Income during the COVID Pandemic," Office of the Parliamentary Budget Officer, July 7, 2020, https://www.pbo-dpb.gc.ca/en/blog/news/RP-2021-014-M--costing-guaranteed-basic-income-during-covid-pandemic--estimation-couts-lies-un-revenu-base-garanti-pendant-pandemie-covid-19

[6] Nasreddine Ammar, Carleigh Busby, and Salma Mohamed Ahmed, "Distributional and Fiscal Analysis of a National Guaranteed Basic Income," Office of the Parliamentary Budget Officer, April 7, 2021. https://www.pbo-dpb.gc.ca/en/blog/news/RP-2122-001-S--distributional-fiscal-analysis-national-guaranteed-basic-income--analyse-financiere-distributive-un-revenu-base-garanti-echelle-nationale

[7] David A. Green, Johnathon Rhys Kesselman, Lindsay M. Tedds, "Covering all the Basics: Reforms for a More Just Society." December 28, 2020. Pp. 206ff. https://bcbasicincomepanel.ca/

[7] Forget, *Basic Income*, 138.

[8] Government of Canada, *Evaluation of the On-Reserve Income Assistance Program*, October 2018, https://www.sac-isc.gc.ca/eng/1557321693588/1557321741537

[9] Eric A. Hanushek and Ludger Woessmann, "The Economic Impacts of Learning Losses," OECD, September 2020, https://www.oecd.org/education/The-economic-impacts-of-coronavirus-covid-19-learning-losses.pdf

A Reader's Guide

As we gathered stories and insights from the people we introduced in these pages, we struggled with some basic questions about the rights and obligations of every member of society. How does the way we move through the world depend on what we've learned from our parents and grandparents, and what are our children and grandchildren, nieces and nephews, and chosen family learning from us? What is a community and how is it different from a crowd of individuals? Even when we thought we understood the assumptions we brought to this study, we were confronted again and again by deeply held attitudes we hadn't acknowledged.

We began this exercise with a strong belief that everyone in a rich country like Canada deserves to live a life that is not constrained by poverty. We believe that a guaranteed basic income that sets a floor below which no one should have to live is both affordable and essential to community well-being. We see basic income as part of a robust social safety net that includes access to good-quality public health care, child care, and education, supports for people with disabilities, and other public goods and services. We also recognize that our social safety net does not function well, that it was never there for some people, and that only by addressing poverty and deprivation through a basic income can we create the kind of robust, inclusive society that creates opportunities for everyone. However, we also have to recognize and address the invisible relationships of power and privilege in our society. Bringing the hidden into the light is not a simple task for anyone.

We believe that the principal barrier to the introduction of basic income in Canada is the challenge each one of us faces, whatever our background, to trust people whose lives are very different from our own. People who have lived complicated lives are understandably cynical about public institutions and the bureaucracies put in place by "experts" who believe they know how people should live their lives. Years of experience have taught them not to trust systems. Similarly, those who are part of the dominant culture rarely understand people who make different decisions than they would make, or who have fewer choices to begin with. This leads bureaucrats to create even more systems designed to force people to make "better" decisions.

Indigenous people have been victimized by coercive bureaucracies for generations, so it is not a surprise that the *Final Report* of the National Inquiry into Missing and Murdered Indigenous Women and Girls recommended a basic income for all Canadians. Similarly, the first call of the Black Lives Matter movement was for a basic income. The more distant anyone is from mainstream culture, the more likely they are to recognize that people need money to address their unique requirements and need to be trusted to make their own decisions.

We've gathered together some of the questions that we've struggled with over the past year, and we've phrased some of them in deliberately provocative ways. We hope you are as uncomfortable thinking about some of them as we have been. Unlike the math textbook you may remember from elementary school, there aren't any answers at the back of the book.

Questions for Consideration

1. Some financially secure people are very generous, donating a great deal of money to charities to help other people. Some of these same people argue against higher taxes to pay for generous social programs designed to help exactly the same people. What, if anything, are the differences between charity and basic income? Is the answer different for the person delivering help and the person receiving help?

2. For a long time, policy-makers have been reluctant to embrace the idea of basic income. It seemed unthinkable—too unconventional. But crises have a way of changing politics overnight. The COVID-19 pandemic revealed to everyone the limitations of our social safety net. Do you think that the pandemic has changed the way poverty is seen in Canada and, if so, will these changes persist as the economy recovers and some of us return to the kinds of lives we used to lead? Has the pandemic made basic income more or less feasible?

3. How might society be different if everyone who needed it could receive a basic income sufficient to meet their basic needs?

4. The version of basic income discussed in this book is sometimes referred to as a "basic income guarantee" or a "guaranteed income." There is another version that has more traction elsewhere in the world, called "universal basic income." In this alternate version, everyone receives the same amount of money each month, no matter how high their income might be. Governments would recover some of the money received by high-income earners through the income tax system. What are some of the advantages and disadvantages of the two different approaches?

5. Some people might argue, as did the Brookings Institution, that "middle class morality" is the route to a healthier, more economically secure life. Decades of social science research have shown that people who finish high school, wait to have children until they are in committed relationships and can afford to provide conventionally comfortable lives for them, and who work full time are happier, healthier, and more financially secure than others. Do policy-makers have a responsibility to design programs to incentivize people to behave in particular ways for their own good?

6. Religious organizations have been heavily involved in charitable outreach to people living with low incomes. In Canada, Christian churches have also been directly involved in the cultural destruction and subsequent poverty of Indigenous populations through the residential school system. Many shelters are run by faith groups; some require those they serve to pray or listen to a sermon before a meal, while others do not. Some proselytize and others do not.

Faith communities are powerful organizations that help to shape social attitudes towards poverty, charity, and merit, both through their explicit teachings and their actions, which are not always consistent with one another. For example, Dorothy Day was the co-founder of the Catholic Workers Movement and lived and worked in hospitality houses for much of her life in the early decades of the twentieth century. She challenged the hierarchy of the Catholic Church, and asked Church officials and laypeople to examine their faith. She is often quoted as saying: "Christ did not talk about the **deserving poor**. He did not come to save those who deserved to be saved. He died for each one…. The gospel takes away our right forever to discriminate between the **deserving** and the **undeserving poor**."

If you are familiar with a faith tradition, what are its teachings about poverty, charity, and merit? If you belong to a faith community, are these teachings consistent with its actions?

7. Basic income is founded on the idea that individual people with access to the appropriate resources can identify and meet their own needs better than anyone else can. Yet no one has suggested that children be given the freedom to make all their own decisions. We expect their parents to make decisions on their behalf. According to the UN Convention on the Rights of the Child, "The child shall have the right to freedom of expression; this right shall include freedom to seek, receive and impart information and ideas of all kinds...." It also recognizes "the right of every child to a standard of living adequate for the child's physical, mental, spiritual, moral and social development." Should children under 18 years old be eligible for a basic income? How could such a program work for children? At what age should permanent wards of Child and Family Services be able to make their own decisions? How can public policies accommodate the different levels of maturity that characterize young adults? Is discretion on the part of administrators important for young adults aging out of foster care? If young people receive a basic income, should there be more conditions on this age group than on older adults?

8. If the bureaucracy surrounding income support programs and the application process were simplified, many people who rely on such support could navigate the system without the help of caseworkers, who spend much of their time dealing with regulations, program interactions, and bureaucracy. In some communities, these government jobs are the only good jobs. What would happen to these workers, and their communities,

if basic income were introduced? Is it reasonable to maintain a bureaucracy so complex that many people do not receive all the benefits to which they are entitled, in order to protect the jobs of caseworkers? If not, how should the interests of caseworkers be protected?

9. Senator Kim Pate has claimed that 80 per cent of incarcerated women are jailed because of "poverty-related crimes." What are "poverty-related crimes" and what does the concept reveal about our attitudes towards those whose financial circumstances make it seem reasonable to act outside the law?

10. Many people find self-esteem and meaning in life from the work they are paid to do. However, there are many other people who find their real purpose in life outside the paid labour market—people who provide unpaid care for other family members, artists and creators, volunteers, community helpers, and others. Historically, some of the most noteworthy contributions to art, literature, and science have come from people who had, for all intents and purposes, a basic income. These people were sometimes aristocrats with family money or creators who had found a patron to buy them the necessary leisure and time to create great works. They did not need to work to pay the rent or put food on the table. (Of course, many aristocrats used their family money in less elevated ways.) Our focus on paid work evolved along with the industrial revolution at the end of the eighteenth century—a very short time ago in the long history of human life on this planet. How might our society be different if everyone had access to a basic income?

11. The year 2020 was characterized not only by the COVID-19 pandemic but also by demonstrations across North America

and around the world protesting the interactions between police and people of colour. Many argue that criminalization is much more complex than simply committing illegal acts. The first call of the Black Lives Matter movement was for basic income. Could basic income actively help to address systemic discrimination or might it be used as a way to avoid the root causes of social injustice?

12. What are the best ways to ensure that victims of intimate partner violence have more autonomy, choice, and independence, both when in an abusive relationship and after? Would a basic income be useful to people in violent relationships, or might receiving a basic income escalate tensions and further endanger people who are already victimized?

13. Many people have lived with violence their whole lives, from their birth families through group homes and foster care, in and out of jail, and with various partners. They have never had a time of calm and stability to learn how to care for and value themselves. This makes them extremely vulnerable to people who would take advantage of them. What programs and services need to be in place to ensure people can protect themselves from further victimization? How can such services be offered without undermining dignity and autonomy?

14. Violence doesn't always mean broken bodies. Many social justice groups, activists, scholars in race and criminology, and Black and Indigenous leaders have argued that public services can be, and often are, provided in ways that harm the people they are intended to help. For example, transgender and racialized people are sometimes denied culturally appropriate health care, Black youth confront racism in school, and Indigenous mothers still lose their infants to foster care at

birth in some provinces. One of the consequences of living in poverty is that access to the resources necessary for survival depends on behaving in ways that are acceptable to the bureaucracies that govern assistance. Is it possible to provide access to the resources people need to survive without intrusive bureaucracies, or is submission to coercive bureaucracies an inevitable consequence of poverty?

15. Sometimes when we think about basic income, we look at it solely from the perspective of people who would benefit from it, or solely from the point of view of taxpayers who would pay for it. Social policy, however, is enacted by governments that are tasked with balancing the interests of different groups. Basic income is controversial because there are inevitable conflicts of interest. One claim often heard from people who have never been in situations where they needed help is that a basic income would be "wasted, or spent on frivolous things." They sometimes argue that it would be better to deliver support through food vouchers that could be used only to buy food or rent paid directly to landlords. Providing evidence that this belief is not true doesn't convince anyone. Policy-makers might find it politically easier to raise levels of support if they agreed to deliver it in the form of food vouchers. Is it ever acceptable to limit the freedom of recipients to spend money however they like, even though this would be seen by most recipients as both degrading and unnecessary? How should a society make these kinds of decisions?

16. The COVID-19 pandemic has highlighted the important role of care work, including uncompensated care work, in society. Why has it taken until now for the public to seriously engage the question of the value of such essential work?

17. COVID-19 was especially devastating in long-term care homes for seniors, and one of the vectors of infection was traced to personal care workers who travelled from institution to institution on public transit, caring for multiple patients under tight time constraints that allowed too little time for proper hygiene. The pay of personal care workers is low, and contracts are often part time and insecure. This, too, is primarily women's work. Poor working conditions in this sector, and in other sectors such as meat-processing plants, demonstrated that the health of each one of us is linked to the health of everyone else in our community. Since the economic well-being of any one of us linked to that of everyone else, how might people whose incomes are high enough that they won't receive a basic income benefit when others in their community have access to a basic income?

18. Some labour economists have expressed the concern that a basic income will "drive women back to the kitchen" because it would allow them to spend their time providing unpaid care for their own children or other family members rather than working for a wage. Others have suggested that women can make their own decisions, that men have children, too, and that a basic income is one way to recognize the important role that unpaid work plays in supporting our society and our economy. Is society necessarily better off if the parent of a young child works for a wage and pays someone else to care for their child? Is the parent better off?

19. Do people with disabilities need intensive case management? What role should a caseworker play in ensuring people receive the benefits to which they are entitled? (A caseworker plays a role distinct from that of a public trustee. All provinces have public trustees who oversee decisions affecting people who

are found not competent to manage their own affairs.) Would someone receiving a basic income still need a caseworker?

20. Provincial income assistance programs pay people with disabilities higher levels of support than people without disabilities. Recipients also receive specific entitlements for costs associated with their disabilities, such as access to assistive devices like hearing aids or wheelchairs. In principle, every Canadian also has access to health care, and everyone on income assistance also receives Pharmacare and dental care. Some people with disabilities face costs associated with their disability, but others do not. Should people with disabilities receive a higher basic income than people without disabilities? How should the appropriate level be determined?

21. According to the Government of Canada, Treaty payments are paid annually, on a national basis, to First Nations people entitled to receive annuities as a result of their bands' signing certain historic treaties with the Crown. These payments are largely ceremonial because the amounts haven't been changed since the treaties were originally signed more than a century ago. First Nations people in bands covered by Treaty 1, for example, each receive $5 a year.[1] These are unconditional payments, based only on Treaty status. Some people have justified basic income as a payment for the resources of the land. Does the structure of Treaty payments constitute a historical precedent for payment of a basic income to First Nations people?

22. It has been suggested that Abraham Maslow's concept of the "hierarchy of needs" was influenced by his contact with Blackfoot spirituality. Cindy Blackstock has noted that Maslow's hierarchy is similar but not identical to the idea of the "breath of life" from First Nations ontology, and that

both are strongly related to the recognition of the importance of the social determinants of health.[2] She argues that Western concepts should be extended to recognize the importance of culture and context and the multiple dimensions of reality, and to place the individual in a relational context. Importantly, she also notes the generational context of well-being by arguing that well-being should be characterized as multi-generational community actualization instead of individual self-actualization. What role, if any, might basic income play in fostering this broader concept of multi-generational community well-being?

References:

[1] Dan Levin, "Canada's Treaty Payments: Meager Reminder of a Painful History," *New York Times*, July 23, 2017, https://www.nytimes.com/2017/07/23/world/americas/winnipegs-treaty-payments-meager-reminder-of-a-painful-history.html#:~:text=WINNIPEG%2C%20Manitoba%20%E2%80%94%20On%20a%20brilliant,Five%20dollars

[2] Cindy Blackstock, "The Emergence of the Breath of Life Theory," *Journal of Social Work Values and Ethics* 8, no. 1 (2011): 1–16.

Additional Resources

For more information and additional readings, please see the following links:
- Basic Income Canada Network: https://www.basicincomecanada.org/resources
- Basic Income Canada Youth Network: https://www.basicincomeyouth.ca/
- Basic Income Earth Network: https://basicincome.org/
- United Nations Sustainable Development Goals: https://www.un.org/sustainabledevelopment/
- United Nations Declaration on the Rights of Indigenous Peoples: https://www.un.org/development/desa/indigenouspeoples/declaration-on-the-rights-of-indigenous-peoples.html
- United Nations Convention on the Rights of the Child: https://www.ohchr.org/documents/professionalinterest/crc.pdf
- *Reclaiming Power and Place: The Final Report of the National Inquiry into Missing and Murdered Indigenous Women and Girls*: https://www.mmiwg-ffada.ca/final-report/
- The Truth and Reconciliation Commission of Canada: http://www.trc.ca/
- United Way can offer in-person poverty simulation workshops for classes or groups. They also have an online simulation calibrated for various cities across Canada, based on realistic costs and challenges: "Make the Month": http://makethemonth.ca/

- "Buy your opportunity" is a challenging group simulation that encourages us to reflect on the language of "choice" and "opportunity": Jonathan Kodet and Dia Mason, "Buy Your Opportunity: An Experiential Consciousness-Raising Workshop Addressing Economic Inequality and Meritocracy," *Radical Pedagogy* 14, no. 1 (2017), http://www.div17.org/wp-content/uploads/Kodet_and_Mason_2017.pdf

Interviewees
- Hailey Cohen, Expert, formerly in CFS care
- Michael Redhead Champagne, Co-founder of Fearless R2W—Circle of Support
- Charity Leonard, Former Executive Director at Youth Employment Services Manitoba
- Vinnie Lillie, Expert, Community Helper, formerly incarcerated
- Shaun Loney, Author, Co-founder of BUILD Inc.
- Senator Kim Pate, Senate of Canada
- Sharon Perrault, Acting Executive Director of John Howard Society of Manitoba
- Sean Sousa, Former Coordinator at Gang Action Interagency Network (GAIN)
- Angela Janeczko, Expert, Coordinator at West Broadway Bear Clan Patrol
- Jean Doucha, Executive Director at Behavioural Health Foundation
- Rick Lees, Former Executive Director of Main Street Project
- Maddy Turbett, Expert, former Child Care Assistant
- Josephine Grey, Human Rights Activist, Community Organizer
- Dr. Susan Prentice, University of Manitoba
- Amanda Robar, Expert, Disability Advocate
- Al Etmanski, Author, Disability Advocate

- Alaya McIvor, Expert, Organizer of the MMIWG2S Annual Mother's Day Memorial Walk
- Leslie Spillett, Knowledge Keeper at Ongomiizwin Indigenous Institute of Health and Healing
- Qajaq Robinson, Commissioner at the National Inquiry into MMIWG
- Deena Brock, Executive Director at Manitoba Association of Women's Shelters
- Angela Braun, Executive Director at Genesis House
- Lisa Carriere, Community Support Manager at North End Women's Resource Centre

Acknowledgment

"Radical trust" is a central theme of this book and a principle that guided our writing and interviewing process. This book would not have been possible without the trust of those who shared their stories with us. We would like to extend our gratitude to Hailey Cohen, Angela Janeczko, Vinnie Lillie, Alaya McIvor, Maddy Turbett, Josephine Grey, and Amanda Robar for allowing us to learn from you. There are also many others who trusted us along the way and helped connect us with the people featured in this book. This includes Dylan Cohen, Sean Sousa, Samantha Pearce, and Leslie Spillett. We also want to thank those working in the field who took the time to share their knowledge and expertise. This includes Michael Redhead Champagne and those at Fearless R2W—Circle of Support, Charity Leonard, Kelsey Evans and folks at Youth Employment Services Manitoba, Darrien Morton and the Housing Solutions WPG team, Daphne Penrose at the Manitoba Advocate for Children and Youth, the folks volunteering at Bear Clan Patrol in the North End, West Broadway, and West End, Shaun Loney, Kim Pate, Sharon Perrault, Jean Doucha, Rick Lees, Deena Brock, Angela Braun, Lisa Carriere, Qajaq Robinson, Jodie Kehl, Susan Prentice, and Al Etmanski. Thanks to Nicole Herpai, who read the first manuscript and provided encouraging comments. We want to thank ARP Books for making this book possible, Irene Bindi for her valuable edits, and Pat Sanders for careful and supportive copyediting.

Evelyn Forget is an economist at the Rady Faculty of Health Sciences at the University of Manitoba. Her research examines the health and social implications of poverty and inequality, and she is often called upon by governments, First Nations, and international organizations to advise on poverty, inequality, health, and social outcomes. Her most recent book is *Basic Income for Canadians: From the COVID-19 Emergency to Financial Security for All.*

Hannah Owczar is a writer and communications specialist in the department of Community Health Sciences at the University of Manitoba. She is a graduate of the Creative Communications program at Red River College, where she majored in journalism. Owczar's work has appeared in several major news outlets in Manitoba, including the *Winnipeg Free Press* and CBC News. She also holds an undergraduate degree in Human Rights from the University of Winnipeg.

Index

2016 Census 74, 82, 131
2018 Winnipeg Street Census 37, 50
2020 Speech from the Throne 100
2SLGBTQQIA 109
abstinence 57, 59
abuse 26, 28, 45, 62, 105, 112, 113, 114, 116
Abuse and neglect 26
abused women 112
abuser 113
abusive relationship 48, 112, 113, 114, 115, 120, 121, 144
abusive situation 112, 113
accommodation 90
activist 67, 106, 136, 144, 151
addiction 48, 49, 50, 51, 52, 53, 55, 56, 57, 60, 70, 105, 106, 120
addiction treatment 52, 53, 120
addiction treatment programs 120
Addictions Foundation of Manitoba (AFM) 53
addictions treatment sector 56
adequate employment 113
administrative capacity 132
administrative processes 36
advocacy groups 41
aging out / aging out of care 12, 38, 41, 42, 44, 46, 47, 133
Ahmed, Salma Mohamed 34, 137
Alberta 46, 68, 84, 87, 88, 101
alcohol 12, 50, 51, 54, 56, 57, 107
Americans 77

Ammar, Nasreddine 34, 137
anti-racist policy 77
applicant 17, 18, 19, 20, 21, 22, 23, 64, 83, 90, 92, 120, 121, 123, 124, 125, 132
Arango, Diana 118
Aron, Nina 86
artist 11, 73, 126, 136, 143
asexual 109
asset limit 97, 124
assistance levels 94
assistive devices 99, 120
asylum seekers 82
at-risk youth 63
Au, Wendy 34, 47
Aurora Recovery Centre 59
authorities 16, 18, 19, 20, 26, 29
autonomy 55, 57, 95, 121, 122, 125, 129, 130, 132, 144
baby boom 31
bank account 54, 112, 124
bankruptcy 134
banks 13, 16, 21, 22, 41, 122, 124, 134
Banting, Keith 87
barriers 30, 43, 52, 60, 82, 98, 113, 136
Barter, Stacy 47
basic bus service 131
basic income 3, 7, 10, 11, 12, 14, 15, 22, 23, 24, 34, 44, 45, 48, 49, 51, 53, 54, 55, 56, 57, 58, 59, 66, 67,

68, 72, 73, 74, 76, 77, 78, 81, 83,
    86, 87, 96, 97, 98, 99, 100, 101,
    109, 110, 114, 115, 116, 119, 121,
    122, 123, 125, 126, 127, 128,
    129, 130, 131, 132, 133, 135, 136,
    137, 138, 139, 140, 142, 143, 144,
    145, 146, 147, 149, 154
basic income experiments 125
Basic Income Guarantee (BIG) 23,
    86, 122, 140
basic infrastructure 120, 131
basic needs 10, 13, 20, 41, 55, 57,
    58, 63, 67, 78, 92, 93, 133, 140
basic social services 120
Bear Clan Patrol 7, 48, 49, 51, 53,
    55, 57, 59, 151
behaviour issues 26
Behavioural Health Foundation
    (BHF) 52
behavioural therapy 55
Beland, Daniel 98, 101, 102
belonging 62, 64
benefit 10, 11, 14, 17, 18, 20, 21, 22,
    23, 27, 61, 64, 70, 72, 73, 76, 81,
    86, 88, 89, 90, 92, 94, 95, 96,
    98, 99, 100, 102, 105, 114, 115,
    119, 120, 122, 123, 124, 128, 131,
    133, 143, 145, 146
Bill C-92 46
bisexual 109
Black and Indigenous
    communities 127
Black and Indigenous leader 144
Black and Indigenous people 77, 127
Black Lives Matter (BLM) 139, 144
Blackfoot 67, 147
Blackfoot spirituality 147
Blackstock, Cindy 35, 67, 70, 147,
    148
Blattman, Christopher 59
Boulanger, Divas 105, 106

Brandon, Josh 47, 58
Braun, Angela 114, 115, 152, 153
breaching parole 60
Breath of Life 70, 147, 148
British and North America 32
British Columbia 45, 46, 51, 54, 55
British Columbia Coroners
    Service 51
broadband Internet service 131
Brock, Deena 111, 112, 115, 152, 153
Brookings Institution 25, 33, 141
Brownell, Marni 34, 47
Burton, Mary Lund 41
BUILD Inc. 64, 151
Building Futures 42
bus ticket 104, 112, 121
Calgary 85, 87
Calls for Justice 109, 110, 111
Campaign 2000 87
Canada 9, 10, 11, 15, 16, 17, 18, 19,
    20, 21, 22, 23, 24, 27, 28, 29, 30,
    31, 35, 46, 47, 51, 58, 64, 68, 69,
    70, 71, 74, 75, 79, 81, 82, 83, 84,
    85, 87, 88, 89, 95, 96, 97, 99, 100,
    101, 102, 103, 104, 106, 109, 110,
    111, 114, 115, 116, 117, 119, 120,
    122, 123, 125, 126, 128, 129,
    130, 131, 132, 136, 137, 138, 139,
    140, 141, 147, 148, 149, 151
Canada Child Benefit (CCB) 18, 97,
    114, 115
Canada Disability Benefit
    (CDB) 100
Canada Emergency Response Benefit
    (CERB) 10, 13, 20, 22, 83, 99,
    100, 123, 124, 125, 128, 130,
    134, 135
Canada Pension Plan (CPP) 17, 19,
    21, 95, 96, 129
Canada Recovery Benefit (CRB) 99
Canada Workers Benefit (CWB) 123

Index   157

Canadian 10, 11, 15, 20, 24, 28, 30, 35, 42, 60, 63, 69, 70, 71, 74, 78, 82, 84, 85, 86, 87, 89, 94, 96, 97, 98, 99, 101, 103, 108, 109, 110, 111, 116, 117, 119, 123, 130, 133, 136, 137, 139, 147, 154
Canadian Association of Elizabeth Frye Societies 60
Canadian Centre for Policy Alternatives Manitoba Office, The 63
Canadian Chamber of Commerce 11
Canadian economy 84
Canadian Femicide Observatory for Justice and Accountability 117
Canadian government 111
Canadian labour market 82
Canadian population 69, 130
Canadian society 109, 133
Canadian system 108
Canadian Women's Foundation 78, 87
Canadians 11, 15, 20, 24, 30, 74, 86, 89, 94, 96, 98, 101, 103, 109, 110, 116, 119, 123, 137, 139, 154
care 7, 9, 10, 11, 12, 13, 17, 18, 19, 20, 22, 23, 24, 26, 27, 28, 29, 31, 32, 33, 34, 35, 36, 37, 38, 39, 40, 41, 42, 43, 44, 45, 46, 47, 61, 62, 64, 68, 72, 75, 76, 78, 79, 80, 81, 83, 85, 87, 89, 95, 99, 104, 111, 113, 114, 120, 121, 122, 126, 127, 129, 130, 131, 132, 133, 134, 136, 138, 142, 143, 144, 145, 146, 147, 151, 153
care work 9, 10, 72, 78, 79, 81, 134, 145, 146
career and education planning 42
caregiver 32, 83
Cargill 84, 87
Cargill meat-packing plants 84
Carriere, Lisa 112, 113, 114, 152, 153
case managers 43
casework 17, 21, 23, 26, 38, 39, 40, 92, 121, 122, 123, 124, 127, 142, 143, 146, 147
caseworker 17, 21, 23, 26, 38, 39, 40, 92, 121, 122, 123, 124, 127, 142, 143, 146, 147
cash benefits 23
cash transfer programmes 115
Catholic Church 141
CBC News 36, 46, 47, 69, 87, 111, 116, 154
CERB applicant 22, 124
ceremony 120
Champagne, Michael Redhead 41, 42, 44, 151, 153
charity 43, 140, 141, 142, 151, 153
Charter of Rights and Freedoms 95
Chartier, Mariette 34, 47
Child and Family Services (CFS) 26, 27, 28, 29, 36, 37, 38, 40, 41, 42, 43, 45, 46, 47, 49, 104, 105, 107, 151
CFS agencies 26
CFS Manual 40, 43, 47
CFS worker 42, 104, 105
child apprehension 41
child care 13, 23, 26, 31, 79, 80, 87, 114, 138, 151
Child Care Human Resources Sector Council 87
child marriage 115
child-care facility 80
childcare 80
children 9, 12, 13, 18, 20, 24, 25, 26, 27, 28, 29, 30, 31, 33, 34, 35, 36, 37, 38, 39, 41, 45, 46, 47, 48, 49, 55, 75, 79, 80, 81, 88, 94, 101,

102, 112, 114, 115, 116, 119, 120, 129, 131, 134, 138, 141, 142, 146, 153
children in custody 28
children involved in both systems 28
children's safety 112
China 81
Christian 141
citizenship 83, 87
civil servant 123
claim denial 124
Clarke, John 86
classism 53
clawback 88, 94. 97
 clawback rates 94
client 17, 21, 38, 50, 53, 56, 122
clinic 16, 90, 122
cocaine 49, 56, 62, 105
coercive bureaucracies 139, 145
coercive social structures 127
Coffee Time 105
Cohen, Hailey 36, 39, 40, 41, 44, 45, 151, 153
colonial history 107
colonial project 108
Colonial systems 108
colonial violence 108
colonialism 29
committed relationships 25, 141
community building 64
Community Financial Counselling Services 42
community groups 63
community members 42
community support manager 112, 152
community supports 69
community work 75
computer equipment 134
Contreras, Manuel 118
conventions 110

coordinated access to social housing 42
corporate crime 125
corporation 126
Correctional Investigator of Canada 69, 70
corrections system 66, 69
costs for shelters 129
costs of living 63
couch surfed 44
COVID-19 9, 13, 19, 20, 22, 72, 79, 85, 86, 87, 99, 100, 123, 128, 134, 135, 137, 140, 143, 145, 146, 154
crack cocaine 105
crack shacks 105
creating incentives 11
creator 126, 143
crime 28, 29, 56, 59, 60, 62, 63, 65, 66, 67, 68, 69, 103, 110, 111, 125, 135, 143
criminal justice 35, 129
 criminal justice costs 129
criminal record 64, 65
criminalization 10, 12, 24, 63, 68, 106 129, 144
criminalization of poverty 129
criminology 144
crisis 24, 73, 86, 108, 110, 112
Crown 147
cultural destruction 141
cultural identity 74
cultural norms 127
cultural rights 74
culture 11, 13, 17, 29, 120, 127, 139, 148
cycle of poverty 89, 94
Daigneault, Pierre-Marc 98, 101, 102
Day, Dorothy 31, 71, 106, 141, 152
daycare centre 79

declarations 110
dedicated supports 120
deep poverty 33, 119
degrading work 73
democracy 64
dental care 23, 147
Department of Families 38, 45, 47, 70, 88, 101
Department of Justice 111, 117, 137
dependence 38, 43, 44, 95, 112, 116, 121, 135, 136, 144
deportation 83, 84
deprivation 29, 33, 138
DeRiviere, Linda 113, 118
deserving poor 141
dignified life 24, 34, 97
dignity 11, 15, 22, 50, 52, 56, 77, 85, 98, 110, 121, 122, 125, 144
direct cash transfer 54
disability 7, 10, 13, 18, 19, 20, 21, 22, 23, 33, 76, 88, 89, 90, 91, 93, 95, 96, 97, 98, 99, 100, 101, 102, 119, 120, 122, 127, 129, 130, 133, 134, 136, 138, 146, 147, 151
disability benefits 88, 95
Disability Policy 88, 101
Disability Support 10, 13, 18, 19, 20, 21, 22, 23, 33, 76, 89, 91, 97, 102, 122, 129
disability system 95
Disability Tax Credit 89, 97, 100
disadvantaged youth 129
discrimination 75, 91, 96, 109, 144
displaced workers 13, 20, 123
dollar 78, 90, 125, 148
domestic abuse survivors 114
domestic violence 108, 114
dominant culture 11, 13, 17, 127, 139
Doucha, Jean 50, 151, 153
Drugging the Poor 51, 59

Eco-Just Food Network 74
economic and social marginalization 109
economic closure 134
economic consequences 74, 134
economic equality 73, 77, 109
economic growth 133
economic health 134, 135
economic independence 116
economic insecurity 10, 11, 73
economic instability 112
economic marginalization 104, 110
economic opportunities 115
economic security 9
economic well-being 134, 146
economics 25
education 13, 20, 23, 26, 27, 30, 31, 34, 38, 41, 42, 47, 59, 68, 73, 82, 83, 87, 94, 107, 113, 120, 121, 129, 130, 131, 132, 134, 135, 137, 138
educational interruption 135
educational outcomes 27
Educational programs 83
educational system 121, 135
Ekuma, Okechukwu 34
Elders 65
elementary school 25, 134, 139
elevated health-care costs 129
Ellsberg, Mary 115, 118
emergency income support 134
emergency program 123
employer 19, 72, 83, 84, 85, 86
employment 10, 17, 18, 19, 20, 37, 42, 43, 49, 61, 63, 64, 65, 72, 73, 84, 88, 91, 101, 106, 107, 113, 114, 123, 124, 128, 151, 153
Employment and Income Assistance (EIA) 20, 49, 88, 114

Employment Insurance (EI) 10, 19, 128
EI payments 19
empowered 44, 109
Enns, Jennifer 34
epilepsy 91, 92, 99
episodic or invisible disabilities 90
equality 35, 59, 73, 77, 81, 95, 98, 109, 110, 135, 150, 154
equality rights 95
equity 96, 110
established immigrants 82
Etmanski, Al 90, 94, 96, 98, 100, 151, 153
exploitation 37, 79, 84, 85, 104, 105, 106, 107
extensions of care 38, 39
Faith communities 141
faith group 11, 141
faith tradition 142
faith-based environment 53
family size 21
fear of retaliation 112
Fearless R2W 41, 42, 44, 151, 153
Fréchette, Jean-Denis 34
federal benefits 89
federal budget 126
federal election 108
federal government 24, 46, 70, 109, 111, 128, 129, 130, 132, 133
federal income support schemes 96
federal inmates 69
female domain 79
female empowerment 116
femicide 111, 117
Final Report 35, 47, 58, 71, 108, 109, 110, 111, 116, 117, 136, 139, 149
financial assistance 125
financial counselling 42, 43
financial freedom 114, 116

financial independence 112
financial issues 112
financial security 67, 86, 136, 137, 154
financial setbacks 24
financial stability 45
financial success 16
financial support 16, 38, 39, 40, 44, 46, 48, 99, 100
firm 16, 65, 124, 134
First Nations 103, 108, 119, 130, 131, 132, 133, 147, 154
First Nations communities 130, 131, 132
First Nations ontology 147
fly-in only 131
food bank 13, 16, 22, 31, 41, 122, 134
food security 74, 131, 132
food vouchers 145
foreign policy 25
foreign workers 82, 87
Forget, Evelyn L. 3, 86, 87, 101, 137, 154
formal education 30
formerly incarcerated people 12, 67
Foster Care 7, 12, 36, 37, 39, 41, 43, 45, 47, 142, 144
Foster Children 37
foster home 36, 37, 39
Francis, David 35
fraud 21, 69, 125, 126
French 16
front-line service 72
front-line worker 72, 134
fundamental right 33, 125
Futures Forward 42, 43, 44
gang 25, 29, 60, 62, 63, 67, 68, 104, 151
Gang Action Interagency Network (GAIN) 67, 151

Index   161

gang life 60, 62
gang membership 104
Garden City Collegiate 36
gay 109
gender 7, 16, 78, 81, 87, 103, 104, 105, 106, 107, 109, 110, 111, 113, 115, 117, 125, 127, 144
gender inequality 81
gender wage gap 81
Gender-Diverse People / Persons / Folks 7, 103, 104, 105, 107, 109, 111, 113, 115, 117
gender-nonconforming people 127
generational context 148
Genesis House 114, 152
Gennari, Floriza 118
genuinely disabled 95
gig economy 20
Gimli, Manitoba 53
girls 35, 37, 69, 71, 103, 104, 106, 108, 109, 111, 116, 117, 118, 136, 139, 149
GoFundMe 93
good public services 127
Google 41
governance 25
government 9, 10, 13, 16, 17, 20, 22, 23, 24, 33, 46, 47, 52, 69, 70, 77, 82, 86, 97, 99, 100, 101, 102, 108, 109, 110, 111, 116, 117, 122, 123, 127, 128, 129, 130, 132, 133, 137, 140, 142, 145, 147, 154
Government of Canada 70, 102, 109, 116, 132, 137, 147
Government of Canada, Department of Families 70
Government of Manitoba 46, 47, 70, 101
Government of Manitoba, Child and Family Services 47

Government of Manitoba, Department of Families 47
Government of Manitoba, Legislative Review Committee 46, 47
Government of Manitoba, The Provincial Offences Act 70
Government paternalism 127
government policy 127
government support 9
Green, David A. 137
Grey, Josephine 74, 151, 153
Greyhound bus 105
Greyhound bus station 105
GST Rebate 24, 123
Guaranteed Basic Income (GBI) 10, 34, 77, 128, 137, 138
Guaranteed Income (GI) 11, 15, 18, 23, 33, 97, 115, 119
Guaranteed Income Supplement (GIS) 18, 36, 38, 39, 45, 46, 47, 56, 84, 85, 88, 89, 97, 100, 119, 130
guaranteed jobs 126
guaranteed livable income 109
guaranteed services 126
guardianship 38
Guenette, Wendy 34, 47
Hanushek, Eric A. 137
harm 22, 53, 56, 57, 58, 59, 76, 95, 99, 108, 120, 125, 126, 144, 147
harm reduction 56, 57, 58, 59
harsh economic times 128
Haskins, Ron 25, 34
Haushofer, Johannes 118
health aids 92
health and learning issues 27
health care 17, 19, 23, 24, 89, 99, 120, 127, 129, 130, 131, 132, 138, 144, 147
health issues 51, 90, 134
health-care clinic 122

health-care costs 129
health-care practitioner 18
health-care system 99, 129
health-care workers 10
healthy communities 129
healthy families 129
healthy people 129
healthy preschool development 28
Herring, Jason 87
hierarchy 67, 141, 147
hierarchy of needs 147
high school 25, 27, 28, 36, 37, 134, 141
high-employment areas 19, 20
high-income 22, 125, 126, 131, 140
high-income country/countries 125, 131
high-income individuals 125, 126
higher education costs 129
higher income household 103
highest-income earners 23
home ownership 94
homeless 37, 39, 40, 42, 44, 45, 48, 49, 50, 52, 54, 59, 105
homelessness 37, 39, 40, 42, 44, 45, 48, 50, 52, 54, 59, 105
homicide 111
homicide rate 111
honour 110, 117
hospital emergency department 135
hospitality house 141
housing 10, 21, 23, 24, 26, 27, 30, 32, 33, 37, 38, 40, 42, 44, 45, 47, 57, 58, 62, 65, 75, 76, 85, 86, 87, 112, 115, 120, 130, 131, 133, 135, 153
housing instability 26, 37, 42
Housing Solutions 42, 47, 153
Hudson, Eishia 69
Human Rights 33, 35, 74, 77, 78, 103, 110, 151, 154

human trafficker 105
human trafficking 104
human trafficking victim 104
illegal tax evasion 126
immigrants 30, 82, 83
Immigration, Refugees and Citizenship Canada 87
implicit biases 127
incarcerated women 143
incarcerated youth 69
incarceration 12, 60, 61, 65, 66, 68, 69, 129
incarceration rates 69
income 3, 7, 10, 11, 12, 14, 15, 16, 17, 18, 19, 20, 21, 22, 23, 24, 26, 27, 28, 30, 31, 32, 33, 34, 44, 45, 48, 49, 50, 51, 53, 54, 55, 56, 57, 58, 67, 68, 72, 73, 74, 75, 76, 77, 78, 79, 80, 81, 82, 83, 84, 86, 87, 88, 89, 90, 94, 95, 96, 97, 98, 99, 100, 101, 102, 103, 104, 106, 108, 109, 110, 112, 113, 114, 115, 116, 118, 119, 120, 121, 122, 123, 124, 125, 126, 127, 128, 129, 130, 131, 132, 133, 134, 135, 136, 137, 138, 139, 140, 141, 142, 143, 144, 145, 146, 147, 148, 149, 154
income assistance 10, 20, 21, 22, 23, 24, 27, 31, 49, 82, 88, 95, 96, 101, 114, 115, 120, 121, 123, 124, 125, 126, 128, 130, 132, 133, 134, 147
income assistance program 22, 120, 147
income assistance system 125
Income insecurity 78, 103, 104, 108, 112
income level 26, 28, 50, 97, 113
income replacement 18, 19, 23
income support 11, 12, 18, 19, 22, 73, 82, 88, 89, 90, 95, 96, 97, 98, 99, 102, 123, 131, 134, 142

income tax 17, 19, 22, 123, 140
income-insecure population 103
income-tested 23, 122
incremental reform 97
independence 38, 43, 44, 112, 116, 121, 144
Independent Investigation Unit of Manitoba 71
Indian Act 108, 109
Indigenization 69
Indigenous 13, 14, 16, 17, 28, 29, 35, 37, 42, 46, 47, 68, 69, 70, 71, 75, 77, 78, 103, 104, 106, 107, 108, 109, 110, 111, 116, 117, 120, 127, 129, 130, 131, 132, 136, 139, 141, 144, 149, 152
Indigenous adults 68
Indigenous communities 29, 110, 127, 129, 130, 132
Indigenous communities and organizations 29
Indigenous governments 17, 132
Indigenous leader 144
Indigenous people / person 13, 28, 46, 68, 69, 70, 77, 107, 108, 109, 110, 120, 127, 130, 131, 139, 149
Indigenous perspective 107
Indigenous sovereignty 120, 132
Indigenous spiritual practices 108
Indigenous trans woman 106
Indigenous women 35, 69, 71, 78, 103, 104, 106, 107, 108, 109, 111, 116, 117, 136, 149
Indigenous women and girls 35, 69, 71, 104, 106, 108, 109, 111, 116, 117, 149
Indigenous youth 42, 47
individual payment levels 98
individual residents of Canada 129
inequality 59, 81, 135, 150, 154
infection 85, 134, 146

informal family-type support 42
infrastructure 31, 120, 131
injustice 14, 144
Inner-city illicit drug use 52
instability 26, 37, 42, 43, 112
institutional care 111
institutionalization 60, 135
institutions 16, 110, 133, 139
insurable 19, 20
intensive case management 146
intergenerational trauma 107
Internet 13, 22, 124, 131, 134
Internet access 22, 124, 134
intersex 109
Intimate Partner Violence (IPV) 111, 115, 117, 118
Inuit 103, 109, 119, 130
investments 31, 55, 94, 131
invisible disabilities 90
isolation 13
Jaiswal, Atul 101
Jamaica 75
Jamison, Julian C. 59
Janeczko, Angela 48, 49, 50, 52, 53, 56, 57, 151, 153
job precarity 74
John Howard Society of Canada, The 71
Jones, Shannon 101
Justice 14, 15, 24, 28, 29, 35, 37, 60, 61, 62, 63, 66, 68, 76, 77, 109, 110, 111, 117, 129, 137, 144
justice system 28, 29, 35, 37, 60, 61, 62, 63, 66, 68, 117
youth justice system 28, 29
Kenya 115, 118
Kesselman, Johnathon Rhys 137
King Jr., Martin Luther 77, 86
Kingston, Ontario 81
kinship support initiative 42
Kiplesund, Sveinung 118

Knowledge Keeper 104, 152
labour 10, 11, 19, 20, 65, 72, 77, 78, 79, 81, 82, 83, 84, 85, 86, 112, 113, 114, 118, 126, 127, 143, 146
labour economist 146
labour legislation 84, 85
labour market 19, 20, 65, 77, 81, 82, 86, 112, 113, 114, 118, 126, 127, 143
labour shortage 84
lack of identification 112
landlord 21, 31, 124, 145
Langara College 45
learning issues 27
learning pod 13
LeDrew, Robin 118
Lee, Janelle Boram 34
Lees, Rick 50, 151, 153
legal infrastructure 31
legal tax loophole 126
legislation 36, 38, 39, 45, 46, 47, 84, 85, 88
Legislative Review Committee 45, 46, 47
Leonard, Charity 43, 151, 153
lesbian 109
Levasseur, Joanne 47
Levin, Dan 148
Liberal government 108
liberal public policy 25
Liberia 55, 59
life transition 121, 131
Lillie, Vinnie 60, 61, 62, 63, 64, 66, 68, 151, 153
livable income 26, 109
live-in caregivers 83
lived experience 49
Local Groups 41
Loney, Shaun 64, 65, 66, 70, 151, 153
long-term care 130, 134, 146

long-term paid employment 91
low income 16, 73, 74, 125, 141
Low Income Families of Toronto (LIFT) 74
low-, middle-, and high-income countries 125
low-employment areas 19
low-income people 123
low-income population 122
low-income residents 23
low-income workers 19, 99
low-paid workers 10
lucky break 32
MacWilliam, Leonard 34, 47
Mager, Zoë 47
Mainstay 58
Malanik-Busby, Carleigh (née Busby) 34, 137
male partner 115
manipulation tactic 115
Manitoba 14, 27, 28, 34, 35, 36, 37, 38, 41, 42, 43, 45, 46, 47, 52, 53, 60, 61, 63, 65, 68, 69, 70, 71, 79, 80, 88, 95, 96, 101, 111, 112, 114, 148, 151, 152, 153, 154
Manitoba Advocate for Children and Youth 47
Manitoba Assistance Act 95, 96
Manitoba Centre for Health Policy 27, 35, 37
Manitoba Department of Families 38
Manitoba government 46
Manitoba's Child and Family Services Standards Manual 38
Manitoba's Department of Families 45
Marcoux, Jacques 71
marginalization 104, 109, 110
marginalized community 77
Maslow, Abraham 67, 147

Maslow's Hierarchy 67, 147
massage parlour 107
maternal poverty 27
McColl, Mary Ann 101
McCulloch, Scott 34
McGregor, Janyce 87
McIvor, Alaya 104, 105, 106, 107, 108, 110, 152, 153
McIvor, Roberta 108
Mckeganey, Neil 59
medical 18, 33, 56, 88, 90, 91, 94, 120, 121, 134
medical care 33, 120, 121, 134
medical diagnosis 90
men 55, 63, 65, 66
mental health 13, 42, 50, 54, 90, 133, 135
mental health counselling 42
mental health issues 90
Métis 103, 109, 119, 130, 131
middle class 25, 33, 34, 50, 141
middle class morality 141
middle-class families 26
middle-class workers 10
migrant workers 82
minimum wage 80, 90
minimum-wage workers 73
minors 69
misogyny 109
missing 35, 62, 63, 69, 71, 103, 104, 105, 106, 107, 108, 111, 116, 117, 136, 139, 149
Missing and Murdered Indigenous Women and Girls [and 2 Spirit People] (MMIWG[2S]) 35, 71, 104, 106, 110, 116, 117, 149, 152
mixed-race person 75
Mlambo-Ngcuka, Phumzile 116
Moderate Alcohol Program (MAP) 56

money 13, 21, 22, 23, 24, 26, 30, 31, 34, 40, 44, 45, 51, 53, 54, 55, 57, 58, 61, 62, 64, 66, 67, 68, 78, 80, 81, 88, 94, 97, 98, 105, 112, 113, 114, 115, 121, 122, 124, 127, 128, 129, 130, 131, 139, 140, 143, 145
monitoring 90, 125
Montreal 31
moral burden 135
Morris, Zoë 59
Morton, Darrian 47, 153
Morton, Matthew 118
Mother's Day Memorial Walk 152
murder 35, 69, 71, 103, 104, 106, 107, 108, 111, 116, 117, 136, 139, 149
Murphy, Caitlin 101
national basic income 130, 132
National Bureau of Economic Research 30
National Inquiry 35, 69, 71, 104, 108, 109, 116, 117, 136, 139, 152
national investigation 111
national program 19, 129
Neale, Jo 59
needs-testing 125
neglected or abused 28
newcomers 16, 73, 74, 86
Newcomers 81, 82
Newfoundland fishing boats 30
Nickel, Nathan Nickel 34
Nino, Christina Maes 47, 58
non-controlling partner 132
non-governmental organizations 16
non-Indigenous person 107, 131
non-Indigenous women 106, 107, 111
non-profit agencies 18
non-profit organizations 41, 42
non-standard contracts 20
non-Status 130, 131

normal economic times 128
norms 127
North End 41, 62, 65, 112, 152, 153
North, The 112, 131, 132, 153
nursing home 9
Oaks, The 59
Old Age Security (OAS) 18, 49, 97, 119
on-reserve 119, 120, 130, 131, 132, 133, 137
online account 123, 124, 130
Ontario 34, 74, 76, 81, 86, 87, 91, 94, 101, 102, 125
Ontario Basic Income Network 74
Ontario Disability Support Program (ODSP) 91, 92, 93, 94, 97, 101, 102
ontology 147
opioid 126
oppressive policies 108
Organization for Economic Co-Operation and Development 35
organized crime 62
Ottawa 56, 59, 87, 132
outlawing of Indigenous spiritual practices 108
Outstanding Warrant Policy 63
over-policing 135
overdose 51, 58
paid labour market 19, 86, 114, 126
pandemic 9, 10, 11, 13, 19, 20, 23, 72, 81, 83, 84, 99, 100, 116, 123, 128, 133, 134, 135, 136, 137, 140, 143, 145
Parliamentary Budget Office (PBO) 24, 34, 125, 128, 137
parole 60, 63
parole officer 63
passive victims 112

Pate, Kim 60, 68, 125, 126, 127, 143, 151, 153
paternalism 125, 126, 127, 136
peer mentors 65
pension 17, 18, 19, 21, 51, 89, 95, 97, 119, 129
people of colour 13, 73, 74, 75, 127, 144
people with disabilities 18, 19, 88, 89, 96, 90, 91, 94, 98, 99, 100, 101, 119, 120, 127, 130, 133, 138, 146, 147
permanent residents 82
permanent ward 36, 37, 38, 142
perpetrated 108, 111
perpetrators 107
Perrault, Sharon 61, 65, 66, 151, 153
persistent poverty 11, 136
personal support workers 72
Pharmacare 22, 147
pharmaceuticals 99, 120
physical abuse 113
physical and mental challenges 28
physical disabilities 90
physical health 134, 135
physical violence 103
police-reported violent crim 111
policing 21, 97, 127, 129, 135
policy 11, 14, 15, 17, 23, 24, 25, 27, 28, 32, 33, 34, 35, 37, 39, 47, 59, 63, 70, 72, 77, 87, 88, 101, 108, 113, 123, 127, 132, 137, 140, 141, 142, 145
policy debate 15, 33
policy maker 14, 17, 33, 34, 123, 140, 141, 145
political parties 85
Pollock, Shoshana 69, 70
poor, the 24, 51, 52, 59, 77, 119
poor mothers 26
poor parents 26

Poor People's Campaign 77
Pope 136
Portage La Prairie 105, 106
post-secondary program 38
potential employers 84
potential trauma 43
poverty 10, 11, 12, 21, 22, 23, 24, 25, 26, 27, 28, 29, 30, 33, 46, 50, 52, 54, 55, 57, 59, 61, 63, 66, 68, 69, 74, 77, 78, 80, 87, 89, 91, 94, 96, 97, 101, 103, 105, 109, 112, 113, 115, 116, 118, 119, 120, 121, 122, 126, 128, 129, 130, 131, 135, 136, 138, 140, 141, 142, 143, 145, 149, 154
poverty is expensive 129
poverty line 11, 12, 21, 22, 24, 33, 80, 89, 97, 113, 119, 120, 121, 122, 128
poverty-related crime 69, 135, 143
power relationships 127
prairie farms 30
prairies 111
precarious employment 73
precarious work 72, 73, 74, 78, 82, 83
  low-paid precarious work 82
precarity 74, 78
predictable income 125
pregnancy 27
prenatal care 27
Prentice, Susan (Dr.) 79, 151
prescription drugs 90
President's Choice 91
prime minister 11, 23, 100
prison 7, 60, 61, 62, 63, 65, 67, 68, 69, 70, 71, 129
prisoner 70
privacy 37, 125
private homes 51, 111
privilege 14, 133, 139

probation 63
probation or parole officer 63
program 11, 12, 16, 17, 19, 20, 21, 22, 23, 24, 31, 38, 43, 45, 53, 56, 57, 58, 63, 76, 80, 82, 83, 85, 86, 88, 89, 90, 91, 94, 95, 96, 97, 101, 102, 113, 115, 118, 119, 120, 122, 123, 128, 129, 131, 133, 137, 140, 141, 142, 144, 147, 154
programs of last resort 120
progressive tax system 22
property 21, 81
proselytize 141
province 20, 22, 24, 28, 36, 45, 46, 52, 53, 68, 82, 83, 87, 88, 89, 90, 95, 96, 111, 112, 122, 126, 128, 129, 130, 133, 145, 146
provincial and territorial governments 70
provincial autonomy 130
Provincial benefits 123
Provincial disability programs 90
provincial disability support 13, 18, 19
provincial income assistance 10, 20, 21, 22, 23, 24, 27, 82, 115, 120, 121, 123, 124, 128, 130, 132, 147
provincial income assistance program 120, 147
provincial jails 70
Provincial Social Assistance 98, 101
provincial tax credits 123
psychological well-being 116
public education 23, 31
Public Health Agency of Canada 103
public policy 25, 32, 33, 34, 127, 137, 142
public programs 31
public service 24, 29, 31, 32, 127, 131, 144

public support 32
public transportation 9, 31, 121
publicly funded services 98
Quebec 89, 119, 129
Quebec Pension Plan 119
queer 13, 109
queer people 13
questioning 109
race 62, 73, 74, 75, 78, 109, 127, 140, 144, 146
racial 16, 73, 78, 110, 119, 125, 127, 144
racialized 16, 73, 78, 110, 119, 127, 144
racialized and Indigenous women 78
racialized people 73, 119, 127, 144
racialized violence 110
racism 29, 73, 75, 78, 109, 144
Radical Trust 1, 3, 10, 11, 12, 14, 18, 20, 22, 24, 26, 28, 30, 32, 34, 38, 40, 42, 44, 46, 50, 52, 54, 56, 58, 62, 64, 66, 68, 70, 74, 76, 78, 80, 82, 84, 86, 90, 92, 94, 96, 98, 100, 102, 104, 106, 108, 110, 112, 114, 116, 118, 120, 122, 124, 126, 128, 130, 132, 134, 136, 140, 142, 144, 146, 148, 150, 152, 153, 156, 158, 160
recidivism 65
Reconciliation 7, 14, 108, 117, 119, 121, 123, 125, 127, 129, 131, 133, 135, 137, 149
Refugees 30, 82, 87
registered First Nations 130
Reid, Colleen 118
reintegrate 60
Religious organization 141
rent 5, 9, 11, 12, 13, 16, 17, 18, 20, 21, 22, 23, 24, 25, 26, 27, 28, 29, 30, 31, 32, 33, 36, 37, 39, 40, 41, 42, 43, 44, 45, 49, 51, 52, 53, 54, 67, 73, 75, 76, 77, 79, 80, 82, 89, 90, 92, 94, 96, 98, 99, 106, 107, 109, 112, 113, 114, 119, 121, 122, 124, 127, 128, 131, 132, 133, 134, 135, 138, 139, 140, 142, 143, 145, 146, 151, 153
rental agreement 40
reoffending 60
Report Card 87, 111, 117
reproductive and home-based care work 81
reserve 81, 119, 120, 130, 131, 132, 133, 137
Resettlement Assistance Program 82
residential school system 29, 108, 141
residential schools 29, 35, 109, 120
residential transition house 42
responsibility 17, 38, 85, 141
risk 10, 28, 38, 50, 55, 56, 57, 63, 72, 78, 83, 89, 90, 94, 103, 104, 107, 112, 119, 124, 134
Robar, Amanda 91, 92, 93, 94, 97, 99, 100, 151, 153
Roberts, Lynn 101
Robertson, Michele 59
Robinson, Qajaq 109, 110, 152, 153
Robson, Jennifer 137
Rousseau, Jean-Jacques 16, 34
Royal Canadian Mounted Police (RCMP) 103, 116
Royal Milk Plant 81, 83
rural 114, 121, 131
rural and remote communities 131
safe and affordable housing 112
safe consumption sites 12, 13, 120
safety and well-being of children 36
safety net 10, 11, 17, 20, 66, 113, 114, 125, 135, 136, 138, 140
Sandy Bay Ojibway First Nation 108
Saskatchewan 68, 111

scholar 67, 69, 101, 144
school-ready 27
school-to-prison pipeline 129
Schultz, Jennifer 34, 47
Schwartz, Saul 137
security 9, 10, 11, 18, 44, 67, 73, 74, 78, 86, 97, 103, 104, 108, 112, 119, 121, 131, 132, 136, 137, 154
Segal, Hugh 87
self-employed 20
self-esteem 65, 67, 126, 143
self-isolated 13
self-reported spousal violence 111
self-respect 95
self-sufficiency 113
self-worth 58
Senate Finance Committee 10, 11
Senior Fellows 25
service dog 92, 93
services 10, 13, 16, 17, 23, 24, 26, 29, 31, 32, 33, 35, 36, 37, 38, 42, 43, 45, 46, 47, 49, 50, 52, 53, 59, 61, 70, 75, 77, 96, 98, 99, 101, 102, 104, 116, 120, 121, 126, 127, 129, 130, 131, 132, 138, 142, 144, 151, 153
settler-colonial 108
settler-colonial system 108
sex industry 44, 104, 105, 106, 107, 110
sex work 106, 113
sex-work activist groups 106
sexual exploitation 104, 105
sexual, emotional, or physical violence 103
Shapiro, Jeremy 118
Sherida, Margaret 59
shutdown 123
Singer, Merrill 51, 52, 59
single mother 49, 119
single parent 76, 119

Sixties Scoop 29, 108, 109, 120
skills building 64
small businesses 134
social assistance 20, 61, 64, 66, 89, 98, 101, 110, 112, 113, 125
Social assistance programs 113
social assistance recipients 89
social assistance system 125
social change 54, 59, 73, 74
social class 51
Social Enterprise 64, 65
social inclusion 64
social justice group 144
social marginalization 109
social policy 24, 145
social program 11, 119, 120, 123, 140
social safety net 10, 11, 17, 20, 113, 125, 135, 136, 138, 140
social science 141
social services 33, 75, 77, 96, 102, 120
social support 43, 129
social systems 75
social worker 39, 42, 43, 136
socio-economic backgrounds 51
socio-economic status 112
sources of income 122
Sousa, Sean 67, 151, 153
sovereignty 120, 132
special needs 23, 49
special-needs children 49
Spillett, Leslie 104, 108, 152, 153
spousal violence 111
St. James Town 74, 75, 86
St. James Town Service Providers' Network 74, 86
stable housing 10, 26
stable support network 43
Stadler, Martin 95, 96, 102

Stadler v Director, St Boniface/
   St Vital (2020) 102
standard immigration quotas 85
standardized tests 27
Statistics Canada 51, 58, 68, 69, 70,
   71, 87, 89, 101, 106, 111, 116, 117
Statistics Canada study 106
status 50, 76, 83, 84, 112, 130, 131,
   147
Steelworkers Union 11, 136
stereotype 95
stress 31, 32, 44, 50, 60, 61, 66, 67,
   80, 114
Structural Determinants of
   Poverty 30
Structural Forces 32
subsidized housing 133
substance abuse 45
substance use 7, 10,12, 27, 44, 48,
   49, 50, 51, 53, 55, 56, 57, 59, 133
substances 50, 57, 120, 127
substandard housing 85, 120
substantive equality 77
supply-chain 134
support network 43, 112
support program 12, 17, 19, 76, 89,
   90, 91, 102, 142
support system 57
supportive housing 120, 130
Supreme Court 96, 102
surveillance 125
survival mode 110
Survival Sex Industry 44, 104, 105,
   106, 107, 110
sustainable development 76, 149
Synod of Anglican Bishops 136
system 13, 14, 17, 22, 24, 25, 26, 28,
   29, 35, 37, 38, 39, 40, 41, 42, 43,
   44, 45, 46, 55, 57, 58, 60, 61, 62,
   63, 66, 68, 69, 73, 75, 78, 90, 91,
   92, 94, 95, 96, 98, 99, 108, 109,
   117, 121, 125, 127, 128, 129, 132,
   135, 139, 140, 141, 142, 144
system navigation 43
systemic change 73
systemic discrimination 91, 144
systems 13, 14, 28, 29, 35, 42, 61,
   68, 75, 96, 108, 139
tax 17, 19, 21, 22, 24, 80, 83, 89, 91,
   97, 100, 123, 124, 125, 126, 129,
   133, 137, 140, 145
tax avoidance 126
tax credit 19, 89, 97, 100, 123
tax evasion 125, 126
tax fraud 125
tax rates 24, 129
tax return 123, 124, 137
tax revenue 126
taxpayers 21, 133, 145
Tedds, Lindsay M. 137
temporary wage subsidies 72
terms and conditions 10
territorial governments 70
territory 36, 88, 126
Toronto, Ontario 31, 74, 86, 101,
   137
total income 82, 131
traditional gender roles 16
trafficked 12
transformational strategy 97
transgender 106, 109, 110, 144
transition plan 38, 39, 46
transportation 9, 26, 31, 40, 93, 121,
   132
trauma 39, 43, 45, 48, 62, 107, 110,
   113, 126
treaties 110, 147
treatment 47, 50, 52, 53, 56, 57, 59,
   107, 120
Treaty Payment 147, 148
true equity 110

Index 171

Truth and Reconciliation Commission (TRC) 108, 117, 149
tuition waiver program 45
Turbett, Maddy 79, 151
Turnbull, Lorna 34
twentieth century 141
Two Spirit / Two-Spirit 103, 104, 106, 108, 109, 110
Two Spirit people / persons 104, 106, 108, 110
Uber 72, 83
Uganda 75
uncertainty 43
unconditional money / support 18, 44
undereducated 55
undeserving poor 141
unemployment 37, 107
United Nations 33, 35, 74, 149
Universal Basic Income (UBI) 22, 140
Universal Declaration of Human Rights (UDHR) 33, 35
University of Manitoba 42, 151, 154
unpaid care 143
unpaid work / labour 9, 77, 79, 118, 146
urban 42, 131
Valdivia, Jeff 34, 47
Vancouver 44, 45, 54
vicious cycle 60
victim 13, 31, 51, 69, 103, 104, 106, 112, 116, 117, 134, 139, 144
victimization 13, 103, 106, 116, 117, 139, 144
victimization rates 106
violence 7, 12, 52, 55, 59, 61, 103, 104, 105, 106, 107, 108, 109, 110, 111, 113, 114, 115, 116, 117, 118, 144

Violence Against Women 7, 103, 105, 107, 109, 111, 113, 115, 116, 117, 118
violent crime 103, 111
violent relationship 112, 144
visas 81, 83, 85
voluntarily leaving 39
volunteer 63, 64, 70, 126, 143, 153
Volunteer Canada 64, 70
volunteer work 63, 64
vulnerable children 28
vulnerable people 10, 73, 81
wage 19, 31, 51, 58, 65, 72, 73, 74, 75, 78, 79, 80, 81, 84, 85, 86, 90, 120, 122, 134, 146
Wall-Wieler, Elizabeth 34
waste-water arrangements 131
Watts, Charlotte 118
we are all in this together 13
weed 62
welfare 20, 29, 35, 37, 41, 42, 45, 46, 47, 70, 90, 91, 101, 102, 113, 120, 125, 126, 132, 136
 Child Welfare 35, 37, 41, 42, 45, 46, 47, 120, 132
welfare assistance 113
welfare fraud 125, 126
welfare programs 113
welfare system 29, 37, 41
well-being 33, 36, 73, 103, 116, 134, 138, 146, 148
well-being of children 36
well-off families 30
Western concepts 148
western Europeans 30
white Canadian 74
willing partner 132
Winnipeg 3, 34, 35, 36, 37, 41, 42, 47, 48, 50, 58, 62, 63, 65, 67, 69, 70, 80, 104, 105, 106, 118, 148, 154

Winnipeg Police Service 69
Winnipeggers 63
Winnipeg's West Broadway
    neighbourhood 48
withdrawal 52, 55, 58
Woessmann, Ludger 137
women 7, 11, 12, 35,53, 62, 69, 70,
    71, 73, 78, 79, 81, 87, 103, 104,
    105, 106, 107, 108, 109, 110, 111,
    112, 113, 114, 115, 116, 117, 118,
    119, 136, 137, 139, 143, 146, 149,
    152
Women Seeking Employment 113
women's economic opportunities 115
women's shelter 111, 112, 116, 152
worker 9, 10, 11, 13, 17, 19, 20, 21,
    22, 23, 26, 35, 38, 39, 40, 41, 42,
    43, 72, 73, 79, 81, 82, 83, 85, 86,
    87, 92, 99, 104, 105, 121, 122,
    123, 124, 127, 133, 134, 136, 141,
    142, 143, 146, 147
workforce 13, 31, 32, 83, 87, 113
workforce goals 113
working 13, 18, 19, 20, 26, 33, 43,
    51, 64, 65, 67, 72, 73, 74, 76, 77,
    79, 80, 81, 84, 86, 88, 89, 94,
    107, 112, 113, 114, 120, 123, 126,
    133, 146, 153
working condition 86, 146
working people 89, 123
working poverty 113
working-age 18, 19, 20, 79, 88, 120
working-age people 18, 19, 88, 120
World Health Organization
    (WHO) 112, 118
young adult 38, 39, 43, 133, 142
young people 12, 44, 73, 142
youth 28, 29, 35, 37, 38, 41, 42, 43,
    44, 45, 46, 47, 63, 69, 70, 71, 129,
    144, 149, 151, 153

Youth Employment Services
    Manitoba 42, 153
youth support worker 41
Zdrill, Kevin 68, 70